Foundations
of Faith

INVITED TO BELIEVE

Student Workbook 2

WP Wheaton Press
Train. Equip. Reflect.

Foundations of Faith
Student Workbook 2

© 2010, 2013, 2015
Published by Wheaton Press
Wheaton, Illinois

www.WheatonPress.com

ISBN-13: 978-0615850856
ISBN-10: 0615850855

1. Christian Education – Discipleship 2. Spiritual Formation – Discipleship. 3. Foundations of Faith – Education. 4. Nonfiction-Religion and Spirituality-Christian Life. 5. Nonfiction-Spiritual Growth-Christ-centered.

Copyright and Trademark Standard

Contact the publisher for discounted copies for partner schools and receive free resources and training for teachers. Learn more at WheatonPress.com or email WheatonPress@gmail.com

FOR OUR CHILDREN.

THESE ARE WRITTEN THAT YOU MIGHT **BELIEVE**

John 20:31, NIV

Foundations of Faith

INVITED TO BELIEVE

Equipping Students to Reflect Christ

	YEAR ONE	YEAR TWO	YEAR THREE	YEAR FOUR
Growth Emphasis	An Emphasis on Believing	An Emphasis on Following	An Emphasis on Loving	An Emphasis on Going
Essential Questions	1. What does a healthy, mature follower of Christ believe? 2. How does a healthy, mature follower of Christ live?	3. How do I grow as a healthy, mature follower of Christ? 4. How do I equip others to grow as healthy, mature followers of Christ?	5. Who do others say Jesus is? 6. Who do I say Jesus is?	7. What do I believe? 8. Why do I believe? 9. How will I communicate to others?
Essential Outcomes	Understand and articulate Christ-centered **beliefs**	Develop authentic Christ-centered **values**	Develop and articulate a Christ-centered **vision**	Develop a clear Christ-centered personal **mission**
Courses	**Foundations of Faith**	**Spiritual Formations** **Leadership, Evangelism, & Discipleship**	**Life of Christ** **Philosophy & Theology**	**Doctrine & Apologetics** **Christ & Culture**

Class Overview

Course Essential Questions

1.   What does a healthy, mature follower of Christ believe?

2.   How does a healthy, mature follower of Christ behave?

Unit Essential Questions

1.   How do I understand the Bible?

2.   How does God reveal His plan from Adam to Abraham?

3.   How does God reveal His plan from Abraham to Moses?

4.   How does God reveal His plan from Moses to David?

5.   How does God reveal His plan from David to Christ?

6.   How does God reveal His plan from Christ to Commission?

7.   How does God reveal His plan from Commission to Culmination?

8.   What do I believe?

Course Description

This class will focus on inviting students to build a solid foundation of belief in the person of Christ and His teachings. Students will examine the Christ centered theistic worldview in comparison to other major worldviews and gain an understanding of what it means to apply God's invitation to love Him with all of their heart, soul, and mind. Students will be challenged to apply the definitions of faith and truth in their examination of the Bible's claim to be God's collected book of inerrant revelation. Ultimately, the course will provide the opportunity to gain an understanding of the whole of Scripture in view of the mission of God.

Learning Outcomes

A.   Define and apply the basic concept of epistemology as it relates to the understanding of faith and truth

B.   Identify the basic elements of a worldview and articulate the differences between materialism, idealism, dualism, and theism

C.   Examine the foundational elements of faith systems and understand the foundational distinctions of a Christ-centered worldview

D.   Examine the distinctly Christian belief that truth is not subjective but defined objectively through the person of Christ (John 14:6)

E.   Learn to integrate and communicate truth in the context of healthy peer dialogue (Hebrews 3:13)

F.   Examine evidence for Christ-centered beliefs and make individual determinations regarding the reliability and trustworthiness of these beliefs

G.   Examine historical and archeological evidence to determine if the Bible can be trusted as the personal revelation of God

H.   Develop and implement a basic apologetic for the reliability of personal belief

Unit 1　How do I understand the Bible?

1. How does a worldview influence how someone views the Bible?

2. How is the Bible organized?

3. Does the Bible prove the existence of God?

4. What is God's mission on earth?

5. How does understanding the mission of God help me understand the Bible?

Unit 2　From Adam to Abraham

1. What does the Bible reveal about creation?

2. What do God's instructions to Adam and Eve reveal about His mission?

3. How did this reality disintegrate?

4. How does understanding the impact of sin equip me to understand reality?

5. How does understanding God's mission influence my understanding of the flood?

6. How does understanding God's mission influence my understanding of Babel?

7. Review: What have I learned?

8. Assessment: How will I demonstrate what I have learned?

9. Assessment review: What do I still need to learn?

Unit 3　From Abraham to Moses

1. Who is Abraham?

2. Who is Ishmael?

3. Who is Isaac?

4. What happened on Mount Moriah?

5. Who is Jacob?

6. How did God use Israel's time in Egypt to advance His mission?

7. Who is Moses?

8. Review: What have I learned?

9. Assessment: How will I demonstrate what I have learned?

Unit 4   From Moses to David

1.   What is the Passover?

2.   How did God turn a multitude into a nation?

3.   What happened on Mount Sinai?

4.   What is the tabernacle?

5.   What is the Day of Atonement?

6.   Who is Joshua?

7.   How does God use the Jordan River and Jericho to reveal glory?

8.   Who is Rahab?

9.   Who is Ruth?

10.   Who is Saul?

11.   Review: What have I learned?

12.   Assessment: How will I demonstrate what I have learned?

Unit 5   From David to Christ

1.   Who is David?

2.   What is God's covenant with David?

3.   Who is Solomon?

4.   What happened to the northern tribes of Israel?

5.   Who are Daniel and Esther?

6.   Who are Ezra and Nehemiah?

7.   Who is Isaiah?

8.   Review: What have I learned?

9.   Assessment: How will I demonstrate what I have learned?

Unit 6   From Christ to Commission

1. Who is Zechariah?

2. Could Jesus have been the Messiah?

3. Did Christ claim to be the Messiah?

4. Did Christ's life meet the messianic standard?

5. Why did Jesus die on a cross?

6. Did Jesus rise from the dead?

7. How do Christ's last words on earth reflect the eternal mission of God?

8. Review: What have I learned?

9. Assessment: How will I demonstrate what I have learned?

10. Extra

Unit 7   From Commission to Culmination

1. What is the church?

2. Who is the Holy Spirit?

3. How will it all end?

4. What have I learned?

Final   What do I believe?

How Do I Understand the Bible?

Foundations of Faith

INVITED TO BELIEVE

Unit Essential Questions

1. How do I view the Bible?

2. How do I understand the Bible?

Unit Learning Objectives

A. To understand the essential questions, learning objectives, and expectations for this class

B. To identify my personal presuppositions toward the Bible

C. To develop a personalized learning plan for this class

D. To apply hermeneutical skills by practicing a word, passage, and concept study

Unit Learning Assessments

1. Word study group project

2. Passage study group project

3. Concept study group project

4. Unit exam

Daily Essential Questions

1. How does a worldview influence how someone views the Bible?

2. How is the Bible organized?

3. Does the Bible prove the existence of God?

4. What is God's mission on earth?

5. How does understanding the mission of God help me understand the Bible?

My Expectations

1. The name that I like to be called is (nickname) _____.

2. The reason that I'm taking this class is because (other than because it's required):

3. One thing that I'm looking forward to in this class is:

4. Two things that I want to learn in this class include:

   1.

   2.

5. One goal that I have for myself this year is:

6. One thing that my teacher could pray for me about this semester would be:

7. My relationship with Jesus up to this point in my life could best be described as:

11

How does my perspective of reality influence how I understand the Bible?
How do I study a verse?
Genesis 1:1

How does the first verse of the Bible address the two elemental components of reality?

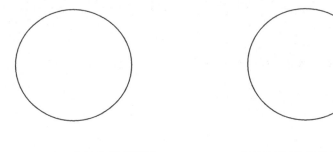

_____   _____

What are the four perspectives of the Bible based on the four foundations of belief?

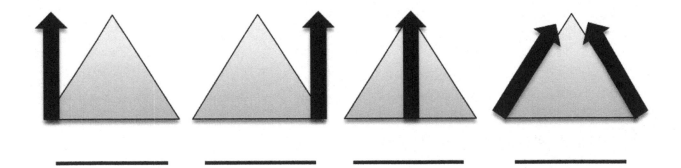

_____   _____   _____   _____

How does a worldview influence how someone views the Bible?

A. Some people approach the Bible as a _____ work of man.

Three reasons why some people approach the Bible as a material work of man include:

      1. They reject the existence of _____ .

         This perspective is called _____ .

            "a" means: "_____"

            Theism means: "_____"

        • An atheist denies the existence of a supernatural God presiding over a natural world.

Turn and Talk: What is the significance of the word *supernatural*?

      2. They reject the ability to _____ God.

         This perspective is called _____ .

            "a" means: "_____"

            Gnostic means: "_____"

        • An agnostic denies the ability to have the knowledge of God.

     3. They reject _____ .

        A.   This could be another form of theism: for example, Islam or Judaism.

            • Other possibilities include cults, like the Jehovah's Witnesses or the Mormons.

        B. This could be a religion representing another worldview. For example:

            • _____ (Idealism)

            • _____ (Dualism)

How does a worldview influence how someone views the Bible?

B. Some people approach the Bible as *containing* the words of man about God.

Turn and Talk: What is the problem with the word *containing*?

Two worldviews that approach the Bible as *containing* the words of man about God include the *deist* worldview and the *emergent* worldview:

1. Deism rejects supernatural involvement.

    Deists believe in the existence of a supernatural creator, but the creator does not _____ with creation. Since deism rejects supernatural involvement or revelation, deists believe that the Bible is man's words written _____ God.

    The deistic rejection of supernatural involvement is another form of materialism.

    Materialists presume material *science** over the possibility of supernatural miracles and _____ .

    A materialist uses the word science *to define "knowledge of any kind."*

    Because deists do not believe in supernatural involvement on the earth, they reject miracles, the resurrection of Christ, and the inspiration of the Bible.

2. Emergents reject _____ and concrete _____ .

    • **What is inerrancy?** Inerrancy is defined as the doctrinal teaching that the Scriptures in the original manuscripts [*autographa*] are true and without error in all that they teach.

    Emergents believe that the Bible is a testimony about the revelation of God through history, but do not believe that it is the unchanging revelation of God.

    Emergents believe that the Bible was written by fallible men and therefore contains errors that are open to cultural interpretation.

    • **What is doctrine?** Doctrine is defined as, a set of _____ .

    Emergents believe that doctrine and beliefs change with culture and context, and as a result, they reject absolute truth.

    Emergents believe that cultural norms regarding morality supersede absolute truths as revealed through the Bible.

How does a worldview influence how someone views the Bible?

C. Christ-centered theists approach the Bible as the _____ _____ of God.

    I.   Christ-centered theists believe the Bible is _____ by God.

        What does the word *inspired* mean (in this context)?

Inspiration is the process where God worked in the hearts of human writers to write down His words. These words are perfect, infallible and trustworthy.

See 2 Timothy 3:16.

2. Christ-centered theists believe the Bible is God's _____ of Himself to His creation.

    A.   The Bible is _____. (It is a historical book).

- The Bible is the history of the _____ .

- The Bible is the history of the _____ .

- The Bible is the history of _____ .

- The Bible is the history of the _____ .

    B.   The Bible is His _____ .

- The Bible is the history of _____ .

- The Bible points to the birth of _____ .

- The Bible tells us the history of the life, death, and resurrection of _____ .

- The Bible equips us to live in light of the life, death, and resurrection of _____ .

Why do we use the term *Christ-centered*?

The Bible is centered on Jesus:

He said to them, "This is what I told you while I was still with you: Everything must be fulfilled that is written about me in the Law of Moses, the Prophets and the Psalms." Luke 24:44, NIV

How does my perspective of reality influence how I understand the Bible?
Can I trust the Bible?

The earliest fragments that we have of the New Testament are in the Koine Greek. The church father Papias, Bishop of Hierapolis, said,

> "Matthew compiled the sayings of Jesus in the Hebrew language and everyone translated as he was able."

Why is this system reliable?

In the time of Christ, following a rabbi and being a disciple meant not simply reflecting the life of the rabbi, but memorizing his words.

As a young boy, Matthew would have been raised in the Jewish oral tradition (memorizing the Old Testament Scriptures).

This fact is evidenced by Matthew's careful connection between his inspired text and the Hebrew Scriptures. But in order to reach the wider population, the Scriptures would soon need to be translated into Greek.

Why should we seek to study and understand the Bible?

"Command and teach these things. Don't let anyone look down on you because you are young, but set an example for the believers in speech, in conduct, in love, in faith and in purity. Until I come, devote yourself to the public reading of Scripture, to preaching and to teaching."

I Timothy 4:11–13, NIV

How often do we simply read rather than study the words of God?

Bible Translations

Date	Translation	Description
250 B.C.	Septuagint	The Hebrew Bible translated into Greek by 70 Jewish Scholars
A.D. 400	Vulgate	First version of the Bible translated into Latin that contained all 66 books
A.D. 1380–1385	John Wycliffe (the Wycliffe Bible)	First to translate the Latin Vulgate into English
1525	William Tyndale	First version of the English Bible translated from original languages and printed on a press.
1611	King James Version	Sponsored (not translated) by King James of England

How is the Bible organized?

The Bible is one _____ book recorded in two _____ .

- Another word for the *testaments* is the word _____ .

- *Canon* means a collection of books that are accepted as _____ .

The Old Testament

The Old Testament canon has _____ individual books that are made up of _____ major types of books and covers more than _____ years of history.

- An easy way to remember how many books are in the Old Testament is to count the number of letters in the word _____ (3) and the number of letters in the word _____ (9).

Historic	Poetic/Wisdom	Prophetic
_____	_____	_____
_____	_____	_____
_____	_____	_____
_____	_____	_____
_____	_____	_____
_____	_____	_____
_____	_____	_____
_____	_____	_____
_____	_____	_____
_____	_____	_____
_____	_____	_____
_____	_____	_____
_____	_____	_____
_____	_____	_____
_____	_____	_____
_____	_____	_____
_____	_____	_____

The first seventeen books of the Old Testament are _____

- These books record the history of the nation of _____ .

- _____ of the books record the primary history.

- _____ of the books repeat or expand on the historical timeline.

The next five books are _____ _____ _____ .

The next seventeen books are _____ .

How is the Bible organized?
The New Testament

The New Testament canon has _____ individual books that are made up of _____ major types of books.

Historical	Pauline Epistles	General Epistles
History of the Life of Christ	**Epistles to Churches**	_____
_____	_____	_____
_____	_____	_____
_____	_____	_____
_____	_____	_____
	_____	_____
History of the Church	_____	_____
_____	_____	_____
	_____	_____
	_____	
	Epistles to Individuals	
	_____	
	_____	
	_____	
	_____	

1.   The first five books of the New Testament are _____ books.

   The first four books are the _____ of the life of Christ.

   These books are known as the _____ because they proclaim the good news regarding the life of Christ.

   The fifth book is the _____ of the early church after Christ.

   The Book of Acts is a historical record and not a _____ treatise.

   The Book of Acts provides a timeline and reference for where many of the remaining books of the New Testament canon occur _____ .

2.   The next thirteen books are the Epistles of _____ .

   The word *epistle* means _____ .

   • These are _____ that Paul wrote to churches and individuals.

   • These letters contain the _____ of the church.

   • The first nine epistles are the major letters to the _____ .

   • The next four epistles are the letters to _____ .

3.   The next nine books are the _____ Epistles.

Turn and Talk: Why does genre matter?

Why does it matter whether or not Acts is viewed as a historical book or a doctrinal book?

Keys to understanding the revelation of God

1. The revelation of God is sufficient.

   - It contains everything that we need. (See 2 Peter 13.)

1. The revelation of God is selective.

   The Bible is the most selective book that has ever been written.

      - It does not tell us everything.

      - It is not exhaustive.

      - It is sufficient.

   Sometimes God will invest several chapters to tell us about one event and then pass over several generations in one sentence.

   Why?
   Because God has a purpose for His revelation.

In the beginning, God.
"In the beginning God created the heavens and the earth." Genesis 1:1, NIV

Does the Bible "prove" the existence of God?

It is important to understand that the Bible does not attempt to prove the existence of God. Instead, the Bible presumes the existence of God.

For example, in Psalm 19:1, David writes;

> "The heavens declare the glory of God; the skies proclaim the work of His hands."
> Psalm 19:1, NIV

This verse, like the very first verse of the Bible, assumes the existence of God—through the evidence of His creation—to be a matter of fact.

In other words, in this verse, there is no argument for His existence; no apologetic for how He arrived onto the scene or what He did prior to His choice to initiate creation; no explanation for His background—just a simple statement of fact.

What is God like?

Volumes of books have attempted to systematically identify and elaborate upon the characteristics of God that are revealed through the pages of Scripture.

There are characteristics that He shares with us and characteristics that are unique to Him, but there are three characteristics of God that are specifically revealed in this first verse of Genesis.

First, God is eternal.

David writes,

> "Before the mountains were born or you had brought forth the whole world, from everlasting to everlasting you are God."
> Psalm 90:2, NIV

Second, God is transcendent.

Being transcendent means that He exists outside of and apart from time and space. He is independent unto Himself, meaning that He is in need of nothing and of no one.

In the description He gives of Himself to Moses at the burning bush, He says,

> **"I AM WHO I AM,"**
> Exodus 3:14, NIV

Third, God is creator.

> "In the beginning God created…"
> Genesis 1:1, NIV

The prophet Isaiah writes,

> "This is what the LORD says, your Redeemer, who formed you in the womb: I am the LORD, **the Maker of all things**, who stretches out the heavens, who spreads out the earth by myself."
> Isaiah 44:24, NIV

According to Isaiah, God is not simply *a* creator, but He is *the* singular creator of all things, both in heaven and on earth.

How can we know what God is like?
"In the beginning God created the heavens and the earth." Genesis 1:1, NIV

A fourth thing that we learn through a basic cross-reference of Genesis 1:1 with John 1:3 is that Jesus is our creator.

The Gospel of John opens by informing us that through Jesus all things were made, and without Jesus, "nothing was made that has been made" (John 1:3, NIV).

That statement informs us that it was Jesus who is being spoken of in both Genesis 1 and Isaiah 44.

John goes on to say:

> "In the beginning was the Word and the Word was with God and the Word was God."
> John 1:1, NIV

According to John 1:1, since Jesus is God, then He is not a created being. The same principle of eternal transcendence applies to Him as God.

God Becomes Flesh

Furthermore, John helps us understand what God is like by informing us that God became flesh and lived among us.:

> "The Word became flesh and made His dwelling among us. We have seen His glory, the glory of the one and only Son, who came from the Father, full of grace and truth."
> John 1:14, NIV

In other words, if we want to get a glimpse of what God is like, we need look no further than when God became flesh and lived in front of our very eyes.

John gives more imagery to this concept of the immaterial becoming material in 1 John 1:1–2.

> "That which was <u>from the beginning</u>, which we have <u>heard</u>, which we have <u>seen</u> with our eyes, which we <u>looked upon</u> and have <u>touched</u> with our hands, concerning the word of life— <u>the life was made manifest</u>, and we have <u>seen</u> it, and testify to it and proclaim to you the eternal life, which <u>was with the Father and was made manifest to us</u> ….."
> 1 John 1:1–2, ESV

John reminds the eyewitnesses that with their own eyes and ears, they had front row seats to the manifestation of God, through His incarnation in the person of Jesus.

Reflection:

What is God's mission on earth?
How do I use a word study to understand a concept?

Numbers 14:21

Many of us are not gripped by an understanding of what God is doing here on this earth. We do not see or understand His overall plan—where He has been and where He is going.

However, if we understand where God is going, then we may better understand what He has done and what He is doing.

When we don't have an understanding of how everything fits together, we may see the Bible not as a connected revelation, but as a disconnected, disintegrated story—one where the God of the Old Testament is somehow different from the God of the New Testament.

When we understand the connections, then we understand the fullness and completeness of God's revelation to us.

What is God's mission on earth?

> "but indeed, as I live, all the earth will be filled with the glory of the LORD."

> Numbers 14:21, NASB

How does understanding the mission of God help us understand the Bible?
How is the Bible organized?

What is the goal of God for the earth?

Why does it matter if we understand the goal of God for the earth?

When we approach Scripture from the perspective of the mission of God, we're equipped to connect the truth of God's revelation, in regards to who He is, who we are, and how we relate to God and His mission for us.

We no longer view Scripture through a disintegrated lens but through a lens of unity and wholeness that places God at the center of His revelation.

A self-centered perspective of Scripture reads the Bible from the perspective of "What's in it for me?" A Christ-centered perspective asks the question, "What is the mission or purpose of God?"

God has a material goal in mind. It is a goal that will be achieved on this earth, not just in part of the earth, but throughout the whole earth.

When we understand God's mission or purpose for the earth, then we can observe the progression of how He reveals Himself and His mission throughout history in the pages of Scripture.

Understanding results in freedom. Freedom results in fruit.

Understanding leads to fruit because, as we grow in confidence about God's overall plan, we grow in confidence in how He has called us to participate in His plan.

> "Jesus knew that the Father had put all things under his power, and that he had come from God and was returning to God; so he got up from the meal, took off his outer clothing, and wrapped a towel around his waist. After that, he poured water into a basin and began to wash his disciples' feet, drying them with the towel that was wrapped around him."
>
> John 13:3–5, NIV

Personal Application

What am I learning?

What am I learning?

Adam to Abraham

Foundations of Faith

INVITED TO BELIEVE

Unit Essential Questions

1. What does God reveal about Himself and His mission in Genesis 1–11?

2. How does Genesis 1–11 apply to my life?

Unit Learning Objectives

A. To gain a basic understanding of the impact and consequences of sin on our perspective of reality

B. To gain a basic understanding of the progressive revelation of God through the time period that connects Adam to Abraham

Unit Learning Assessments

1. Interview reflection paper and presentation

2. Written reflection assessment

3. Exam

Daily Essential Questions

1. What does the Bible reveal about creation?

2. What do God's instructions to Adam and Eve reveal about His mission?

3. How did reality disintegrate?

4. How does understanding the impact of sin equip me to understand reality?

5. How does understanding God's mission influence my understanding of the flood?

6. How does understanding God's mission influence my understanding of Babel?

7. Review: What have I learned?

8. Assessment: How will I demonstrate what I have learned?

9. Assessment Review: What do I still need to learn?

From Adam to Abraham
Genesis 1–11

Now that we have seen where God is going, we can trace His steps through His historical narrative as He moves toward that goal.

Genesis 1–11 is the first section of the Word of God. There are 12 recognizable sections of content that reflect one story in the first 11 chapters.

1. Genesis 1 informs us of how God creates, and then how God rests.

   - God creates the heavens and the earth.

   - God creates the immaterial and the material.

1. Genesis 2:7 informs us that God creates humanity.

   - God plants the seed for the purpose of humanity in Genesis 1:26–27 and then expands upon creation in chapter 2.

1. Genesis 3 informs us of how we disregarded our purpose.

1. Genesis 4 informs us of the story of Cain.

   - Cain turns away from God and then turns away from his brother.

1. Genesis 5–6 informs us of the generations from Adam to Noah.

1. Genesis 6:5 and 6:12 inform us of the wickedness of the human heart and how far we have turned away from the glory of God. God tells Noah to build an ark (of atonement), and then He destroys all of the people on the earth who have turned from their purpose of reflecting His glory.

2. Genesis 8 informs us of the flood.

1. Genesis 9 informs us of a new beginning after the flood.

2. Genesis 10 informs us of the generations after the flood through the sons of Noah: Shem, Ham, and Japheth.

3. Genesis 11:1–9 informs us of the tower of Babel.

   Keep in mind that it is the purpose of the tower, not the tower itself, that matters. This is another story about how humans reject the glory of God by striving "to make a name for ourselves."

4. Genesis 11:10 informs us of the genealogy from Shem to Abraham.

What does the Bible reveal about creation?
How do I understand and make sense of the creation narrative?
Genesis 1:1–25, Job 38

Genesis 1:1–25, NASB

[1]In the beginning God created the heavens and the earth. [2]The earth was formless and void, and darkness was over the surface of the deep, and the Spirit of God was moving over the surface of the waters.

[3]Then God said, "Let there be light"; and there was light. [4]God saw that the light was good; and God separated the light from the darkness. [5]God called the light day, and the darkness He called night. And there was evening and there was morning, one day.

[6]Then God said, "Let there be an expanse in the midst of the waters, and let it separate the waters from the waters." [7]God made the expanse, and separated the waters which were below the expanse from the waters which were above the expanse; and it was so. [8]God called the expanse heaven. And there was evening and there was morning, a second day.

[9]Then God said, "Let the waters below the heavens be gathered into one place, and let the dry land appear"; and it was so. [10]God called the dry land earth, and the gathering of the waters He called seas; and God saw that it was good.

[11]Then God said, "Let the earth sprout vegetation, plants yielding seed, and fruit trees on the earth bearing fruit after their kind with seed in them"; and it was so. [12]The earth brought forth vegetation, plants yielding seed after their kind, and trees bearing fruit with seed in them, after their kind; and God saw that it was good. [13]There was evening and there was morning, a third day.

[14]Then God said, "Let there be lights in the expanse of the heavens to separate the day from the night, and let them be for signs and for seasons and for days and years; [15]and let them be for lights in the expanse of the heavens to give light on the earth"; and it was so. [16]God made the two great lights, the greater light to govern the day, and the lesser light to govern the night; He made the stars also. [17]God placed them in the expanse of the heavens to give light on the earth, [18]and to govern the day and the night, and to separate the light from the darkness; and God saw that it was good. [19]There was evening and there was morning, a fourth day.

[20]Then God said, "Let the waters teem with swarms of living creatures, and let birds fly above the earth in the open expanse of the heavens." [21]God created the great sea monsters and every living creature that moves, with which the waters swarmed after their kind, and every winged bird after its kind; and God saw that it was good. [22]God blessed them, saying, "Be fruitful and multiply, and fill the waters in the seas, and let birds multiply on the earth." [23]There was evening and there was morning, a fifth day.

[24]Then God said, "Let the earth bring forth living creatures after their kind: cattle and creeping things and beasts of the earth after their kind"; and it was so. [25]God made the beasts of the earth after their kind, and the cattle after their kind, and everything that creeps on the ground after its kind; and God saw that it was good.

Observations:

Read   What does it say?

Reflect   What does it mean?

Respond   How does it apply?

How long did people live?

Person	Years	Genesis Reference
Adam	930	5:5
Seth	912	5:8
Methuselah	969	5:27
Noah	950	9:29
Shem	600	11:10–11
Eber	464	11:16–17
Peleg	239	11:18–19
Nahor	148	11:24–25
Terah	205	11:32
Sarah	127	23:1
Abraham	175	25:7
Isaac	180	35:28–29
Jacob	147	47:28
Joseph	110	50:26

In the beginning, God created the heavens.

Genesis 1:1

What happened when God created the heavens?

When God created the heavens, He created angels.

What does the Bible tell us about the angels?

A. Angels present themselves to God (Job 2:1).

B. Angels observed the creation of the world (Job 38:4–7).

C. Angels are created a little higher than man (Psalm 8:5).

D. Angels are stronger and more powerful than man (2 Peter 2:11).

E.   Angels do the bidding of God (Psalm 103:20).

F. Angels praise God (Psalm 148:2).

G. Angels will someday be ordered by God to separate the wicked from the righteous in preparation for the judgment of God (Matthew 13:49).

H. Angels do not marry or procreate (Matthew 22:30).

I.   Angels will someday be ordered by God to gather the elect (Matthew 24:31).

J.   There are more than 12 legions of angels (Matthew 26:53, Revelation 5:11).

K.   The angels will be with Christ when He returns (Mark 8:38).

K.   Angels are not to be worshipped (Colossians 2:18).

K.   The angels are created beings who are inferior to the incomparable, uncreated Son of God (Hebrews 1:5).

K.   The angels worship Jesus (Hebrews 1:6).

K.   Angels serve those who inherit salvation (Hebrews 1:14).

K.   Angels are present on earth (Hebrews 13:2).

Who is the enemy of God?
How do I study a passage?
Ezekiel 28:11–19, Isaiah 14:12–15

[11]"Again the word of the LORD came to me saying,

[12]"Son of man, take up a lamentation over the king of Tyre and say to him, 'Thus says the Lord GOD,
" You had the seal of perfection,
Full of wisdom and perfect in beauty.

[13]"You were in Eden, the garden of God;
Every precious stone was your covering:
The ruby, the topaz and the diamond;
The beryl, the onyx and the jasper;
The lapis lazuli, the turquoise and the emerald;
And the gold, the workmanship of your settings and sockets,
Was in you.
On the day that you were created
They were prepared.

[14]"You were the anointed cherub who covers,
And I placed you there.
You were on the holy mountain of God;
You walked in the midst of the stones of fire.

[15]"You were blameless in your ways
From the day you were created
Until unrighteousness was found in you.

[16]"By the abundance of your trade
You were internally filled with violence,
And you sinned;
Therefore I have cast you as profane
From the mountain of God.
And I have destroyed you, O covering cherub,
From the midst of the stones of fire.

[17]"Your heart was lifted up because of your beauty;
You corrupted your wisdom by reason of your splendor.
I cast you to the ground;
I put you before kings,
That they may see you.

[18] "By the multitude of your iniquities,
In the unrighteousness of your trade
You profaned your sanctuaries.
Therefore I have brought fire from the midst of you;
It has consumed you,
And I have turned you to ashes on the earth
In the eyes of all who see you.

[19]"All who know you among the peoples
Are appalled at you;
You have become terrified
And you will cease to be forever.'"'"

Ezekiel 28:11–19

[12]"How you have fallen from heaven,
O star of the morning, son of the dawn!
You have been cut down to the earth,
You who have weakened the nations!

[13]"But you said in your heart,
'I will ascend to heaven;
I will raise my throne above the stars of God,
And I will sit on the mount of assembly
In the recesses of the north.

[14]"I will ascend above the heights of the clouds;
I will make myself like the Most High.'

[15]"Nevertheless you will be thrust down to Sheol,
To the recesses of the pit.

Isaiah 14:12–15, NASB

Observations:

Read   What does it say?

Reflect   What does it mean?

Respond   How does it apply?

When God created the heavens, He also created Lucifer.

What does the Bible tell us about Lucifer?

A. Lucifer was created (Ezekiel 28:13).

Why does it matter that Lucifer was created by God?

The answer is crucial to understanding the difference between a dualist (who would believe that Jesus and Satan are equals) or a Christ-centered theist (who recognizes Satan as a created being).

The implications affect everything from how we view the atonement ("Jesus beating Satan" vs. the penal substitutionary view) to how Mormonism views Christ as Satan's half-brother.

B. Lucifer was anointed as a guardian cherub (Ezekiel 28:14).

C. Lucifer was the model of perfection (Ezekiel 28:12).

D. Lucifer was full of wisdom and perfect in beauty (Ezekiel 28:12).

E. Lucifer was in the garden of Eden (Ezekiel 28:13).

F. Lucifer was blameless from his creation until the time of his sin (Ezekiel 28:15).

G. Lucifer was driven from the mount of God in disgrace (Ezekiel 28:16).

H. Lucifer sinned by becoming proud (Ezekiel 28:17).

I. Lucifer was punished by being thrown to the earth in front of the rest of the angels (Ezekiel 28:17, Isaiah 14:12).

J. One third of the angels followed Lucifer in his sin (Revelation 12:4).

K. Lucifer sinned in his heart with five "I will" statements (Isaiah 14:13–14).

1. I will ascend to heaven.
2. I will raise my throne above the stars [angels] of God.
3. I will sit on the throne in the assembly [of the angels].
4. I will ascend above the heights of the clouds.
5. I will make myself like the Most High [God].

Why are these statements significant?

The answer is crucial to our understanding of our own sin. Every day, our own pride puts us on the throne of our life and invites us to follow our own will, rather than God's will for our lives.

What is the effect of Lucifer's sin?

- The eternal fire has been prepared for Lucifer, the angels who followed him, and anyone who does not follow Christ.

    Matthew 25:41

- Angels who followed Lucifer in his sin are destined to hell.

    2 Peter 2:4

    Jude 1:6

- Lucifer (Satan) must still present himself before the Lord in subjection.

    Job 1:6–7

- Lucifer has still been allowed limited and temporary power on the earth.

    Job 1:12

    Matthew 4:1–3, 5, 8, 10–11

- Lucifer is the enemy of those who side with his enemy.

    1 Peter 5:8

- Lucifer and the demons who follow him are still scheming about how to devour and attack followers of Christ.

    Ephesians 6:11–12

- Lucifer will ultimately be crushed under the feet of those who follow Christ.

    Romans 16:20

In the beginning, God created the heavens and the earth.

Genesis 1:1

What happened when God created the earth?

A. God created animals (Genesis 1:24–25).

- God made the birds and fish (Genesis 1:20–22).

- God made the land animals (Genesis 1:24–25).

- Animals were initially created to be vegetarians (Genesis 1:30).

B. God created humans (Genesis 1:26–27).

Humans initially lived in the garden of Eden (Genesis 2:8).

The garden of Eden was located at the headwaters of four major rivers. Two of those rivers were named the Tigris and the Euphrates (Genesis 2:14).

Humans are created to reflect the image of God (Genesis 1:26).

Humans are created distinct from the animals and other creation because humans bear the image of God (Genesis 5:1).

- Adam is the father of all humanity (1 Corinthians 15:45, 1 Timothy 2:13).

- Eve is the mother of all humanity (Genesis 3:20).

- Humans were initially created to be vegetarians (Genesis 1:29).

- Man and woman were created to be married (united together) in one flesh, both naked and unashamed (Genesis 2:23–25).

- Adam was tasked to work and keep the garden (Genesis 2:15).

- Adam was instructed not to eat of the tree of the knowledge of good and evil (Genesis 2:16–17).

    - The consequence for disobedience would be death (Genesis 2:17).

- Humans are created a little lower than the angels (Hebrews 2:7).

- Humans were created to reflect the glory of God. We are put on display so that our lives will reflect His glory (1 Corinthians 4:9, Ephesians 3:10).

- Humans will someday judge the angels (1 Corinthians 6:3).

Five perspectives on creation:

Atheistic Evolution	Theistic Evolution	Day-Age Theory	Gap Theory	6 Day Creation Theory
Define:	Define:	Define:	Define:	Define:
Strengths:	Strengths:	Strengths:	Strengths:	Strengths:
Weaknesses:	Weaknesses:	Weaknesses:	Weaknesses:	Weaknesses:
Scriptural Support:	Scriptural Support:	Scriptural Support:	Scriptural Support:	Scriptural Support:
Scientific Support:	Scientific Support:	Scientific Support:	Scientific Support:	Scientific Support:

What do God's instructions to Adam and Eve reveal about His mission?
How does the mission of God apply to my life?
Genesis 1:26–31, 2:15–25

Genesis 1:26–31, NASB

²⁶Then God said, "Let Us make man in Our image, according to Our likeness; and let them rule over the fish of the sea and over the birds of the sky and over the cattle and over all the earth, and over every creeping thing that creeps on the earth." ²⁷God created man in His own image, in the image of God He created him; male and female He created them. ²⁸God blessed them; and God said to them, "Be fruitful and multiply, and fill the earth, and subdue it; and rule over the fish of the sea and over the birds of the sky and over every living thing that moves on the earth." ²⁹Then God said, "Behold, I have given you every plant yielding seed that is on the surface of all the earth, and every tree which has fruit yielding seed; it shall be food for you; ³⁰and to every beast of the earth and to every bird of the sky and to every thing that moves on the earth which has life, I have given every green plant for food"; and it was so. ³¹God saw all that He had made, and behold, it was very good. And there was evening and there was morning, the sixth day.

Genesis 2:15–25, NASB

¹⁵Then the LORD God took the man and put him into the garden of Eden to cultivate it and keep it. ¹⁶The LORD God commanded the man, saying, "From any tree of the garden you may eat freely; ¹⁷but from the tree of the knowledge of good and evil you shall not eat, for in the day that you eat from it you will surely die."

¹⁸Then the LORD God said, "It is not good for the man to be alone; I will make him a helper suitable for him." ¹⁹Out of the ground the LORD God formed every beast of the field and every bird of the sky, and brought them to the man to see what he would call them; and whatever the man called a living creature, that was its name. ²⁰The man gave names to all the cattle, and to the birds of the sky, and to every beast of the field, but for Adam there was not found a helper suitable for him. ²¹So the LORD God caused a deep sleep to fall upon the man, and he slept; then He took one of his ribs and closed up the flesh at that place. ²²The LORD God fashioned into a woman the rib which He had taken from the man, and brought her to the man.

²³The man said,

"This is now bone of my bones,
And flesh of my flesh;
She shall be called Woman,
Because she was taken out of Man."

²⁴For this reason a man shall leave his father and his mother, and be joined to his wife; and they shall become one flesh. ²⁵And the man and his wife were both naked and were not ashamed.

Observations:

Read   What does it say?

Reflect   What does it mean?

Respond   How does it apply?

Notes and Discussion:

37

How did reality disintegrate?
What can I learn and apply from the sin of Adam and Eve?
Genesis 3:1–13, NASB

¹Now the serpent was more crafty than any beast of the field which the LORD God had made. And he said to the woman, "Indeed, has God said, 'You shall not eat from any tree of the garden'?" ²The woman said to the serpent, "From the fruit of the trees of the garden we may eat; ³but from the fruit of the tree which is in the middle of the garden, God has said, 'You shall not eat from it or touch it, or you will die.'"

⁴The serpent said to the woman, "You surely will not die! ⁵For God knows that in the day you eat from it your eyes will be opened, and you will be like God, knowing good and evil." ⁶When the woman saw that the tree was good for food, and that it was a delight to the eyes, and that the tree was desirable to make one wise, she took from its fruit and ate; and she gave also to her husband with her, and he ate. ⁷Then the eyes of both of them were opened, and they knew that they were naked; and they sewed fig leaves together and made themselves loin coverings.

⁸They heard the sound of the LORD God walking in the garden in the cool of the day, and the man and his wife hid themselves from the presence of the LORD God among the trees of the garden. ⁹Then the LORD God called to the man, and said to him, "Where are you?" ¹⁰He said, "I heard the sound of You in the garden, and I was afraid because I was naked; so I hid myself." ¹¹And He said, "Who told you that you were naked? Have you eaten from the tree of which I commanded you not to eat?" ¹²The man said, "The woman whom You gave to be with me, she gave me from the tree, and I ate." ¹³Then the LORD God said to the woman, "What is this you have done?" And the woman said, "The serpent deceived me, and I ate."

Observations:

Read   What does it say?

Reflect   What does it mean?

Respond   How does it apply?

Observations:

What was the process and impact of human sin?

A. Adam is instructed not to eat of the tree. (Genesis 2:16–17)

B. Eve is tempted by the serpent to question the word of God and His instructions. (Genesis 3:1)

C. Eve looks at the tree and is tempted with the desire for what three things? (Genesis 3:5–6)

- Pleasure
- Wisdom
- To become like God

D. Adam takes the fruit of the tree from his wife and eats it. (Genesis 3:6)

Notes and Discussion:

E. One of the results of their sin is that they become shameful of their nakedness. (Genesis 3:7)

F. One of the results of their sin is that Adam and Eve attempt to hide from God. (Genesis 3:7–8)

G. One of the results of their sin is conflict and blame within the relationship between husband and wife and their relationship with God. (Genesis 3:12)

H. One of the results of sin is that labor for both men and women would become painful. (Genesis 1:16, 17, 19)

I. One of the results of sin is the production of thorns and thistles, which previously did not exist. (Genesis 1:18)

J. One of the consequences of the serpent tempting Adam and Eve to sin is his eventual destruction and the crushing of his head under their feet. (Genesis 3:15)

How does understanding the impact of sin equip me to understand reality?
What is the relationship between evil and grace?
Genesis 3:15–24, NASB

¹⁵And I will put enmity
Between you and the woman,
And between your seed and her seed;
He shall bruise you on the head,
And you shall bruise him on the heel."

¹⁶To the woman He said,
"I will greatly multiply
Your pain in childbirth,
In pain you will bring forth children;
Yet your desire will be for your husband,
And he will rule over you."

¹⁷Then to Adam He said, "Because you have listened to the voice of your wife, and have eaten from the tree about which I commanded you, saying, 'You shall not eat from it';
Cursed is the ground because of you;
In toil you will eat of it
All the days of your life.

¹⁸"Both thorns and thistles it shall grow for you;
And you will eat the plants of the field;

¹⁹By the sweat of your face
You will eat bread,
Till you return to the ground,
Because from it you were taken;
For you are dust,
And to dust you shall return."

²⁰Now the man called his wife's name Eve, because she was the mother of all the living.

²¹The LORD God made garments of skin for Adam and his wife, and clothed them.

²²Then the LORD God said, "Behold, the man has become like one of Us, knowing good and evil; and now, he might stretch out his hand, and take also from the tree of life, and eat, and live forever"— ²³therefore the LORD God sent him out from the garden of Eden, to cultivate the ground from which he was taken.

²⁴So He drove the man out; and at the east of the garden of Eden He stationed the cherubim and the flaming sword which turned every direction to guard the way to the tree of life.

Observations:

What does it say?

What does it mean?

How does it apply?

What is sin, how did it occur, and what are its consequences?

Prior to sin, man and woman experienced an "integrated" life. **(Integrated:** *whole, complete, authentic, not false.)*

Natural man and woman lived in authentic relationship with each other and with our supernatural Creator.

In this perfect relationship with God, it was common for Him to walk in the garden and enjoy the integrity of a whole, real, and authentic relationship with Adam and Eve. In addition, there was no shame separating Adam and Eve (Genesis 2:25).

Adam and Eve had only the knowledge of goodness, and they reflected the character and image of God. Life between the material and immaterial was perfectly integrated, according to the design of the Creator.

Pause and consider:

> What would it have been like to experience an integrated, whole life?
>
> **(Disintegrate:** *to break up into small parts, typically as the result of impact or decay; to separate.)*

The willful rebellion (sin) of Adam and Eve—choosing their will over the will of the supernatural God who created them—resulted in the disintegration not only of the relationship between God and humanity, but the literal disintegration of *reality* as well.

For the first time, the material and the immaterial—the natural and the supernatural—experienced separation. What was once whole was immediately broken into parts, and as a result, creation began to experience decay.

> He [Adam] answered, "I heard you in the garden, and I was afraid because I was naked; so I <u>hid</u>."
> Genesis 3:10, NIV

- One of the first consequences of sin is that natural humans experienced a separation from the supernatural Creator.

- There was literally a disintegration of reality in its most elemental form.

- A separation occurred, as the relationship between the material and immaterial was broken.

How does understanding the impact of sin equip me to understand reality?
Genesis 3:15–24

What is sin, how did it occur, and what are its consequences?

We have continued to experience the results of this initial separation, or disintegration, with every continuing generation since the original sin of Adam and Eve. As each generation gets further and further away from God's original intention, the results of the decay is evidenced throughout physical and relational reality.

This is what the Bible means when it says,

> "…for all have sinned and <u>fall short</u> of the <u>glory</u> of God."
> Romans 3:23, NIV

Perhaps you have read this particular verse so many times that it has become meaningless.

Many of us have been taught that we are separated from God and that we need Jesus to forgive us from our sin, but we have wondered if things are really that bad. After all, many of us seem to be nice people.

- Does the separation between God and humanity and the continuing disintegration and decay of reality really affect our day-to-day lives?

- Beyond our need for Jesus to save us from hell, how bad is the impact of our disintegration on our daily lives?

What does the Bible say?

> "The god of this age has <u>blinded the minds</u> of unbelievers, so that they cannot see the light of the gospel that displays the glory of Christ, who is the image of God."
> 2 Corinthians 4:4, NIV

The disintegration of reality that separated the material from the immaterial has left unbelievers with blinded minds. The result is an inability to see the glory of Christ (who is the perfect reality) and who reflects the image of God.

What is the solution?

> "And we all, who with unveiled faces contemplate the Lord's
> glory, are being transformed into his image with ever-increasing
> glory, which comes from the Lord, who is the Spirit."
>
> 2 Corinthians 3:18, NIV

According to the Bible, once a person becomes a believer in Christ, he or she not only experiences the justification that comes with the forgiveness of sins, but is also able to contemplate the glory of God and begin the process of being transformed into His reflection.

Seeing reality from a Christ-centered perspective not only equips individuals to make sense of life, but it provides the hope of returning to authentic wholeness.

> "Therefore we do not lose heart. Though outwardly we are
> wasting away, yet inwardly we are being renewed day by day. For
> our light and momentary troubles are achieving for us an eternal
> glory that far outweighs them all."
>
> 2 Corinthians 4:16–17, NIV

Making sense of the world:

Consider how many other verses begin to make sense when we view the world through a Christ-centered worldview, understanding the theological implications of our sin and why we live in a disintegrated reality.

> "So we fix our eyes not on what is seen, but on what is unseen,
> since what is seen is temporary, but what is unseen is eternal."
>
> 2 Corinthians 4:18, NIV

Making sense of worldviews:

Take a close look at the words that Paul uses in Colossians 2:8. Recognize how Paul acknowledges the fragmented (disintegrated) worldviews and compares them to the fullness of a Christ-centered worldview.

> "See to it that no one takes you captive through hollow and
> deceptive philosophy, which depends on human tradition
> [material] and the elemental spiritual forces [immaterial] of this
> world rather than on Christ [100% Material and Immaterial]."
>
> Colossians 2:8, NIV

How does understanding God's mission influence my understanding of the flood?
Genesis 6:5–22, 7:1–5, NASB

[5]Then the LORD saw that the wickedness of man was great on the earth, and that every intent of the thoughts of his heart was only evil continually. [6]The LORD was sorry that He had made man on the earth, and He was grieved in His heart.

[7]The LORD said, "I will blot out man whom I have created from the face of the land, from man to animals to creeping things and to birds of the sky; for I am sorry that I have made them." [8]But Noah found favor in the eyes of the LORD.

[9] These are the records of the generations of Noah. Noah was a righteous man, blameless in his time; Noah walked with God. [10]Noah became the father of three sons: Shem, Ham, and Japheth.

[11]Now the earth was corrupt in the sight of God, and the earth was filled with violence. [12]God looked on the earth, and behold, it was corrupt; for all flesh had corrupted their way upon the earth.

[13] Then God said to Noah, "The end of all flesh has come before Me; for the earth is filled with violence because of them; and behold, I am about to destroy them with the earth. [14]Make for yourself an ark of gopher wood; you shall make the ark with rooms, and shall cover it inside and out with pitch.

[15]This is how you shall make it: the length of the ark three hundred cubits, its breadth fifty cubits, and its height thirty cubits. [16]You shall make a window for the ark, and finish it to a cubit from the top; and set the door of the ark in the side of it; you shall make it with lower, second, and third decks.

[17]Behold, I, even I am bringing the flood of water upon the earth, to destroy all flesh in which is the breath of life, from under heaven; everything that is on the earth shall perish. [18]But I will establish My covenant with you; and you shall enter the ark—you and your sons and your wife, and your sons' wives with you. [19]And of every living thing of all flesh, you shall bring two of every kind into the ark, to keep them alive with you; they shall be male and female.

[20]Of the birds after their kind, and of the animals after their kind, of every creeping thing of the ground after its kind, two of every kind will come to you to keep them alive. [21]As for you, take for yourself some of all food which is edible, and gather it to yourself; and it shall be for food for you and for them." [22]Thus Noah did; according to all that God had commanded him, so he did.

Genesis 6:5–22, NASB

The Flood

[1]Then the LORD said to Noah, "Enter the ark, you and all your household, for you alone I have seen to be righteous before Me in this time. [2]You shall take with you of every clean animal by sevens, a male and his female; and of the animals that are not clean two, a male and his female; [3]also of the birds of the sky, by sevens, male and female, to keep offspring alive on the face of all the earth.

[4]For after seven more days, I will send rain on the earth forty days and forty nights; and I will blot out from the face of the land every living thing that I have made." [5]Noah did according to all that the LORD had commanded him.

Genesis 7:1–5, NASB

Genesis 7:6–24, NASB

[6]Now Noah was six hundred years old when the flood of water came upon the earth. [7]Then Noah and his sons and his wife and his sons' wives with him entered the ark because of the water of the flood. [8]Of clean animals and animals that are not clean and birds and everything that creeps on the ground, [9]there went into the ark to Noah by twos, male and female, as God had commanded Noah. [10]It came about after the seven days, that the water of the flood came upon the earth. [11]In the six hundredth year of Noah's life, in the second month, on the seventeenth day of the month, on the same day all the fountains of the great deep burst open, and the floodgates of the sky were opened. [12]The rain fell upon the earth for forty days and forty nights.

[13]On the very same day Noah and Shem and Ham and Japheth, the sons of Noah, and Noah's wife and the three wives of his sons with them, entered the ark, [14]they and every beast after its kind, and all the cattle after their kind, and every creeping thing that creeps on the earth after its kind, and every bird after its kind, all sorts of birds. [15]So they went into the ark to Noah, by twos of all flesh in which was the breath of life. [16]Those that entered, male and female of all flesh, entered as God had commanded him; and the Lord closed it behind him.

[17]Then the flood came upon the earth for forty days, and the water increased and lifted up the ark, so that it rose above the earth. [18]The water prevailed and increased greatly upon the earth, and the ark floated on the surface of the water. [19]The water prevailed more and more upon the earth, so that all the high mountains everywhere under the heavens were covered. [20]The water prevailed fifteen cubits higher, and the mountains were covered. [21]All flesh that moved on the earth perished, birds and cattle and beasts and every swarming thing that swarms upon the earth, and all mankind; [22] of all that was on the dry land, all in whose nostrils was the breath of the spirit of life, died.

[23]Thus He blotted out every living thing that was upon the face of the land, from man to animals to creeping things and to birds of the sky, and they were blotted out from the earth; and only Noah was left, together with those that were with him in the ark. [24]The water prevailed upon the earth one hundred and fifty days.

Genesis 7:6–24, NASB

Genesis 8:1–12

[1]But God remembered Noah and all the beasts and all the cattle that were with him in the ark; and God caused a wind to pass over the earth, and the water subsided. [2]Also the fountains of the deep and the floodgates of the sky were closed, and the rain from the sky was restrained; [3]and the water receded steadily from the earth, and at the end of one hundred and fifty days the water decreased. [4]In the seventh month, on the seventeenth day of the month, the ark rested upon the mountains of Ararat. [5]The water decreased steadily until the tenth month; in the tenth month, on the first day of the month, the tops of the mountains became visible.

[6]Then it came about at the end of forty days, that Noah opened the window of the ark which he had made; [7]and he sent out a raven, and it flew here and there until the water was dried up from the earth. [8]Then he sent out a dove from him, to see if the water was abated from the face of the land; [9]but the dove found no resting place for the sole of her foot, so she returned to him into the ark, for the water was on the surface of all the earth. Then he put out his hand and took her, and brought her into the ark to himself. [10]So he waited yet another seven days; and again he sent out the dove from the ark.

[11]The dove came to him toward evening, and behold, in her beak was a freshly picked olive leaf. So Noah knew that the water was abated from the earth. [12]Then he waited yet another seven days, and sent out the dove; but she did not return to him again.

Genesis 8:1–12, NASB

How does understanding God's mission influence my understanding of the flood?

What is God's covenant with Noah? Genesis 8:13–21, 9:1–14, NASB

[13]Now it came about in the six hundred and first year, in the first month, on the first of the month, the water was dried up from the earth. Then Noah removed the covering of the ark, and looked, and behold, the surface of the ground was dried up. [14]In the second month, on the twenty-seventh day of the month, the earth was dry.

[15]Then God spoke to Noah, saying, [16]"Go out of the ark, you and your wife and your sons and your sons' wives with you. [17]Bring out with you every living thing of all flesh that is with you, birds and animals and every creeping thing that creeps on the earth, that they may breed abundantly on the earth, and be fruitful and multiply on the earth."

[18]So Noah went out, and his sons and his wife and his sons' wives with him. [19]Every beast, every creeping thing, and every bird, everything that moves on the earth, went out by their families from the ark. [20]Then Noah built an altar to the Lord, and took of every clean animal and of every clean bird and offered burnt offerings on the altar. [21]The Lord smelled the soothing aroma; and the Lord said to Himself, "I will never again curse the ground on account of man, for the intent of man's heart is evil from his youth; and I will never again destroy every living thing, as I have done.

Genesis 8:13–21, NASB

How long was Noah in the ark?

7 Days	Noah and his family enter the ark seven days prior to the flood.
40 Days	Rains and flooding
150 Days	Water recedes until the ark rests on Arafat
178 Days	Water continues to recedes until Noah and his family disembark

375 Total Days

[1]And God blessed Noah and his sons and said to them, "Be fruitful and multiply, and fill the earth. [2]The fear of you and the terror of you will be on every beast of the earth and on every bird of the sky; with everything that creeps on the ground, and all the fish of the sea, into your hand they are given.

[3]Every moving thing that is alive shall be food for you; I give all to you, as I gave the green plant. [4]Only you shall not eat flesh with its life, that is, its blood. [5]Surely I will require your lifeblood; from every beast I will require it. And from every man, from every man's brother I will require the life of man.

[6]"Whoever sheds man's blood,
By man his blood shall be shed,
For in the image of God
He made man.

[7]"As for you, be fruitful and multiply;
Populate the earth abundantly and multiply in it."

[8]Then God spoke to Noah and to his sons with him, saying, [9]"Now behold, I Myself do establish My covenant with you, and with your descendants after you; [10]and with every living creature that is with you, the birds, the cattle, and every beast of the earth with you; of all that comes out of the ark, even every beast of the earth. [11]I establish My covenant with you; and all flesh shall never again be cut off by the water of the flood, neither shall there again be a flood to destroy the earth." [12]God said, "This is the sign of the covenant which I am making between Me and you and every living creature that is with you, for all successive generations; [13]I set My bow in the cloud, and it shall be for a sign of a covenant between Me and the earth. [14]It shall come about, when I bring a cloud over the earth, that the bow will be seen in the cloud . . .

Genesis 9:1–14, NASB

Notes and Discussion:

Observations:

Read   What does it say?

Reflect   What does it mean?

Respond   How does it apply?

How does understanding God's mission influence my understanding of Babel?
Why does God scatter the people at Babel?
Genesis 11:1–9, NASB

[1]Now the whole earth used the same language and the same words. [2]It came about as they journeyed east, that they found a plain in the land of Shinar and settled there. [3]They said to one another, "Come, let us make bricks and burn them thoroughly." And they used brick for stone, and they used tar for mortar.

[4]They said, "Come, let us build for ourselves a city, and a tower whose top will reach into heaven, and let us make for ourselves a name, otherwise we will be scattered abroad over the face of the whole earth." [5]The Lord came down to see the city and the tower which the sons of men had built.

[6]The Lord said, "Behold, they are one people, and they all have the same language. And this is what they began to do, and now nothing which they purpose to do will be impossible for them. [7]Come, let Us go down and there confuse their language, so that they will not understand one another's speech.

[8]So the Lord scattered them abroad from there over the face of the whole earth; and they stopped building the city. [9]Therefore its name was called Babel, because there the Lord confused the language of the whole earth; and from there the Lord scattered them abroad over the face of the whole earth.

Observations:

Read   What does it say?

Reflect   What does it mean?

Respond   How does it apply?

Notes and Discussion:

There are three major parts to the first eleven chapters of Genesis.

Each of the three major parts is divided by a section of genealogy:

Part I. Chapters 1–4

- Chapter 5 (the descendants of Adam)

Part II. Chapters 6–9

- Chapter 10 (the descendants of Noah)

Part III. Chapter 11a

- Chapter 11b (the descendants of Shem)

There are three things that God reveals through this prologue:

1. God's original purpose for mankind and our disobedience. (Genesis 1–4)

God created us to be in relationship with Him and to reflect His glory, but we turned our backs on Him, breaking the relationship and reflecting our own glory instead. (Genesis 1–4)

2. The corruption and destruction of mankind. (Genesis 6–9)

God restarts not with two people but with eight. He is increasing His glory.

3. God's desire was to fill the earth with His glory, but our desire was to stay in one place. (Genesis 11)

Summary: What is God doing?

God creates. God reveals His plan. God maintains His plan to fill the earth with His Glory.

Perhaps the emphasis in the first eleven chapters is not on what God is doing, but on the story of how mankind responds to what God desires to do. Is it possible that God is laying out our response to His goal, apart from His plan (as revealed in Genesis 12)?

Genesis 1–11

- God's purpose is to fill the earth with His glory.
- God made mankind (men and women) in His image.
- Mankind rebelled.
- Mankind filled the earth with his/her own glory, rather than God's glory.
- Mankind would not scatter.
- God initiated His plan.

Review:
What have I learned?
Genesis 1–11

The Foundational Questions	How does Genesis 1–11 address the foundations of faith?
1. What is real?	
2. Who/what is God?	
3. Who is man?	
4. What is moral?	
5. What happens at death?	
6. What is the meaning of history?	
7. Why are we here?	

Abraham
to Moses

Foundations of Faith

INVITED TO BELIEVE

Unit Essential Questions

1. How does God reveal and accomplish His mission from the time of Abraham through Moses?

2. How does understanding the progression of God's plan from Abraham to Moses impact my life?

Unit Learning Objectives

A. To understand how God continues to advance His mission to reflect His glory to the ends of the earth by initiating a covenant with Abraham

B. To examine the principle that while God is sufficient and sovereign, He is not always efficient in His processes

Unit Learning Assessments

1. Formative Quizzes

2. Summative Assessment

Daily Essential Questions

1. Who is Abraham?

2. Who is Ishmael?

3. Who is Isaac?

4. What happened on Mount Moriah?

5. Who is Jacob?

6. How did God use Israel's time in Egypt to advance His mission?

7. Who is Moses?

8. Review: What am I learning?

9. Assessment: How will I demonstrate what I have learned?

From Abraham to Moses

The greatest break in Scripture occurs between Genesis 11 and 12. God begins something in chapter 12 that we do not see prior to this point: God never claims to be the God of Adam, but He regularly claims to be the the God of Abraham, Isaac and Jacob. The story of God's mission moves from one man to the creation of one nation that will be commissioned to reflect the glory of God to a watching world.

In Genesis 12, God initiates a part of His eternal plan for reflecting His glory. It is not about what Abraham or the Jewish people will do, but what God will do through Abraham and the nation of Israel.

The key to understanding this concept is the four words found at the beginning of God's covenant promise to Abram: "I will make you…"
(Genesis 12:1, NIV).

God acts in ways that we do not, so that we know it is He who does it.

Events in the life of Abraham	Age	Genesis Reference
Leaves Ur	?	11:31
Covenant with God	75	12:1–9
Moves to Egypt; lies to Pharaoh about his wife	?	12:10–20
Covenant renewed by God	?	15
Birth of Ishmael	85	16
Covenant of circumcision	99	17:1–14
Birth of Isaac	100	21:1–7
Mount Moriah: Isaac and the ram in the bush	?	22
Sarah dies	137	23
Finds a wife for Isaac	?	24
Abraham dies	175	25:7–11

What is the story of God's promise to Abraham?

Abraham was human, just like you and me. There was nothing special about him. The beauty of the story of Abraham is that it was not because of Abraham's righteousness that God approached him, but because of God's grace.

The principle of God's grace applies to our lives as well. Every one of us is dead in our own sin and in our own rebellion to God, but it is because of God's grace that He approaches us.

At the time God approached Abraham, he was an idol worshiper and was worshiping false gods.

But God approaches him in Genesis chapter 12 and makes several promises.

The first promise is that Abraham will become a great nation. The irony of this promise is that Abraham and his wife are getting old, and they have no children. The principle and application is that many times God makes us promises and then asks us to have faith to trust him for the outcome.

The second promise is that Abraham will be blessed and that he will have a great name.

The third promise is that Abraham will be a blessing to all people. A study of the history of the Jewish nation shows that this promise has been kept in every aspect of life. Most importantly, however, this is a prophetic reference to Jesus coming as the Messiah from the line of Abraham.

53

What is the story of God's promise to Abraham?

The next promise is that those who bless Abraham will be blessed and those who curse Abraham will be cursed.

This promise is a prophetic reference that is revealed throughout the history of the Jewish nation. A study of the countries who bless the Jewish people reveals that when a nation blesses the nation of Israel, their economy grows and they experience a time of blessing as a nation. History also reveals that as soon as a nation begins to implement ghettos (a ghetto is a place that separates Jewish people from other members of the community), implement pogroms, or deport Jewish people out of their country, their economy, and everything with it, begins to decline.

The last promise is a direct reference to the person of Christ.

Throughout history, there have been people who have understood this covenant, but there have also been times and seasons when, even in the church, this covenant has not been fully understood or recognized.

For example, sadly—and ironically—the first display at the Holocaust Museum in Jerusalem reveals the sad history of Christians who have misused and misapplied this covenant of God with the people of Israel. Some will say that God has now replaced the nation of Israel (with Christians) and the promises that He made to them now belong to the Christian church. This theological view is called replacement theology.

Unfortunately, we are living in a generation where this view is beginning to gain a new following. But as followers of Christ, it is important for us to study what Paul writes in the book of Romans, where he clearly states that God has not forsaken His covenant with His people Israel.

This promise can be seen in Romans 11:1–2a:

> 1"I ask, then, has God rejected his people? By no means! For I myself am an Israelite, a descendant of Abraham, a member of the tribe of Benjamin. 2God has not rejected his people whom he foreknew."
>
> Romans 11:1–2a, ESV

Paul then repeats himself, just a few verses later:

> 11"So I ask, did they stumble in order that they might fall? By no means! Rather through their trespass salvation has come to the Gentiles, so as to make Israel jealous. 12Now if their trespass means riches for the world, and if their failure means riches for the Gentiles, how much more will their full inclusion mean!"
>
> Romans 11:11–12, ESV

Finally, in the last few verses of chapter 11, Paul writes,

> 30"Just as you who were at one time disobedient to God have now received mercy as a result of their disobedience, 31so they too have now become disobedient in order that they too may now receive mercy as a result of God's mercy to you."
>
> Romans 11:30–31, NIV

The key to understanding all of this is knowing that God is the one who is sovereign and in control.

He keeps his promises, and He has not replaced Israel with anyone else.

His promise to Abraham, made in Genesis 12, is the promise that He will keep through all time.

Who is Abraham?
What is God's covenant with Abraham?
Genesis 12:1–3, NASB

Now the LORD said to Abram,
"Go forth from your country,
And from your relatives
And from your father's house,
To the land which I will show you;

And I will make you a great nation,
And I will bless you,
And make your name great;
And so you shall be a blessing;

And I will bless those who bless you,
And the one who curses you I will curse.
And in you all the families of the earth will be blessed."

Observations:

God approaches Abram and makes an unconditional promise (Genesis 12:1–3):

1. Abram will become a great nation.

2. Abram will be blessed.

1. Abram will have a great name.

1. Abram will be a blessing.

1. Those who bless Abram will be blessed.

2. Those who curse Abram will be cursed.

3. All of the people of the earth will be blessed through Abram.

Who is Ishmael?
What is God's covenant with Ishmael?
Genesis 16, NASB

¹Now Sarai, Abram's wife had borne him no children, and she had an Egyptian maid whose name was Hagar. ²So Sarai said to Abram, "Now behold, the LORD has prevented me from bearing children. Please go in to my maid; perhaps I will obtain children through her." And Abram listened to the voice of Sarai.

³After Abram had lived ten years in the land of Canaan, Abram's wife Sarai took Hagar the Egyptian, her maid, and gave her to her husband Abram as his wife. ⁴He went in to Hagar, and she conceived; and when she saw that she had conceived, her mistress was despised in her sight. ⁵And Sarai said to Abram, "May the wrong done me be upon you. I gave my maid into your arms, but when she saw that she had conceived, I was despised in her sight. May the LORD judge between you and me."

⁶But Abram said to Sarai, "Behold, your maid is in your power; do to her what is good in your sight." So Sarai treated her harshly, and she fled from her presence.

⁷Now the angel of the LORD found her by a spring of water in the wilderness, by the spring on the way to Shur. ⁸He said, "Hagar, Sarai's maid, where have you come from and where are you going?" And she said, "I am fleeing from the presence of my mistress Sarai."

⁹Then the angel of the LORD said to her, "Return to your mistress, and submit yourself to her authority." ¹⁰Moreover, the angel of the LORD said to her, "I will greatly multiply your descendants so that they will be too many to count."

¹¹The angel of the LORD said to her further,

"Behold, you are with child,
And you will bear a son;
And you shall call his name Ishmael,
Because the LORD has given heed to your affliction.
¹²"He will be a wild donkey of a man,
His hand will be against everyone,
And everyone's hand will be against him;
And he will live to the east of all his brothers."

¹³Then she called the name of the LORD who spoke to her, "You are a God who sees"; for she said, "Have I even remained alive here after seeing Him?" ¹⁴Therefore the well was called Beer-lahai-roi; behold, it is between Kadesh and Bered.

¹⁵So Hagar bore Abram a son; and Abram called the name of his son, whom Hagar bore, Ishmael. ¹⁶Abram was eighty-six years old when Hagar bore Ishmael to him.

Observations:

What is Abraham's response to the promise of God?

If the story of God's covenant with Abraham is a story of God's faithfulness to His promises, then it is also a story of our unfaithfulness and rebellion against His promises and His grace.

While God is making His promise to Abraham, his wife Sarah overhears the angel of the LORD making the promise, and she begins to laugh. To her it is not only ironic, but it is impossible for a woman of her age to have children. Before we judge Sara for her lack of faith, though, it is important to understand the culture and context she is coming from.

Sarah is the wife of a wealthy landowner. Since she has not yet given birth to a son, she has failed to provide her husband with an heir to his fortune. Without a child, Abraham does not have an heir to pass all of his wealth to.

This situation makes Sarah a woman who feels great shame on a daily basis.

She's accustomed to being talked about by her servants and by the other women who see her. She's a woman who has dealt with a lot of pain and embarrassment, because in her culture, the fact that she is unable to bear a child is considered her fault.

Consider the story from Sarah's perspective: three strange men come to her tent and make her husband an outlandish promise, one that—in her mind—is now impossible to keep.

Most likely, she had finally come to a point in life where she had made peace with the fact that she would never have the child she truly longed for.

So while she is laughing on the outside, most likely this reaction is masking a great pain on the inside; in her mind, she dares not hope for a child again.

Most likely she has wrestled with hope and disappointment before. Though not recorded in Scripture, it is likely that others have promised her special cures designed to ensure that she would become pregnant. Yet every one of those attempts has failed.

Likely, she is now at a point in life where her hope has given way to despair, and her despair has ended in a form of acceptance (or at least an appearance of acceptance).

The promise is made and more time passes.

It is during this time that Sarah gets an idea that perhaps she can help herself, her husband, and this "new" God who has made this "crazy" promise.

She approaches her husband and offers him the opportunity to sleep with her servant Hagar for the purpose of impregnating her rather than continuing to wait any longer for God's promise to be fulfilled.

Abraham agrees to Sarah's proposal, and Abraham and Hagar have a son, whose name is Ishmael. Sarah gets jealous and begins mistreating Hagar and her son.

As Ishmael begins to grow older and time passes, God fulfills His promise and Sarah gets pregnant.

Observations:

What happened?

Abram sins and fathers a child with an Egyptian slave, named Hagar, rather than waiting for the promise of God to be fulfilled through his wife Sarai (Genesis 16:1–4).

a. Hagar becomes pregnant with a son, is mistreated by a jealous Sarai, and runs away (Genesis 16:8).

b. God makes a promise to Hagar regarding her son, Ishmael (Genesis 16:9–13).

     I.   Ishmael will become the father of a _____ _____ .

     II.   Ishmael will be a wild _____ of a man.

     III.   Ishmael will be against _____ (his brothers).

     IV.   _____ would be against Ishmael.

     V.   Ishmael's descendants will live in hostility toward the descendants of _____ _____ .

The Family Tree:

Family Tree		
Isaac		Ishmael
Jacob (Israel)	Esau	
The	**The**	**The**
_____	_____	_____
Jacob has 12 sons who become the 12 tribes of Israel	The nation of Edom expanded and reigned prior to any Israelite king reigning (Genesis 36:31).	
	Edomites	
	Esau marries Oholibamah, the daughter of Anah, the daughter of Zibian the Hivite, who is a grandson of Ham, son of Noah (Genesis 36:2, 1 Chronicles 1:8,13–15).	Esau marries Ishmael's daughter Mahalath (Basemath). (Genesis 36:3).

Who are the descendants of Ishmael?

There are many different thoughts on who the Ishmaelites have become. One theory is that they are Muslims, the modern followers of Muhammad.

Others believe that they are modern-day Palestinians.

Either way, the continued struggle and strife between those who are the children of Abraham through Isaac and those who are the children of Abraham through Ishmael can be traced back to the prophetic promise from God to the two sons of Abraham.

Muslims, who follow Allah, believe that Ishmael is the son of the promise through his mother Hagar. Jews, who are from the nation of Israel, believe that God's promise was made specifically to Abraham and to his wife, Sarah.

Christ-centered theists, who believe in the New Testament, also believe that God made his promise to Abraham and Sarah.

This struggle between brothers can be traced in Scripture through the family of Esau, who married a daughter of Ishmael. Their children became known as the Edomites.

A word study through Scripture of the Edomites continues the story of how the consequences of Abraham's actions have continued to have an impact on later generations.

Collective Applications

- Application I

- Application II.

Personal Application:

What can we learn from Abraham's response to the promise of God?

While the relationships among Abraham, Sarah, Isaac, and Ishmael have many theological and practical applications, for the purposes of today, there are two questions we can ask ourselves:

- What are God's promises to us?

- What is our response to His promises?

It would be a tragedy to miss the underlying story of the faithfulness and trustworthiness of God in this story of pain and impatience.

Ask God to show you areas where the truths from this passage apply to your own life.

Where has God made promises in the midst of your pain?

Has your response been to rest patiently in His timing or to impatiently attempt to help Him out?

Who is Isaac?
How does God renew His promise?
Genesis 17:1–22, NASB

Now when Abram was ninety-nine years old, the LORD appeared to Abram and said to him,

"I am God Almighty;
Walk before Me, and be blameless.

2"I will establish My covenant between Me and you, And I will multiply you exceedingly.

3Abram fell on his face, and God talked with him, saying,

4"As for Me, behold, My covenant is with you, And you will be the father of a multitude of nations.

5"No longer shall your name be called Abram, But your name shall be Abraham; For I have made you the father of a multitude of nations.

6I will make you exceedingly fruitful, and I will make nations of you, and kings will come forth from you. 7I will establish My covenant between Me and you and your descendants after you throughout their generations for an everlasting covenant, to be God to you and to your descendants after you. 8I will give to you and to your descendants after you, the land of your sojournings, all the land of Canaan, for an everlasting possession; and I will be their God."

9God said further to Abraham, "Now as for you, you shall keep My covenant, you and your descendants after you throughout their generations. 10This is My covenant, which you shall keep, between Me and you and your descendants after you: every male among you shall be circumcised. 11And you shall be circumcised in the flesh of your foreskin, and it shall be the sign of the covenant between Me and you. 12And every male among you who is eight days old shall be circumcised throughout your generations, a servant who is born in the house or who is bought with money from any foreigner, who is not of your descendants.

13A servant who is born in your house or who is bought with your money shall surely be circumcised; thus shall My covenant be in your flesh for an everlasting covenant. 14But an uncircumcised male who is not circumcised in the flesh of his foreskin, that person shall be cut off from his people; he has broken My covenant."

15Then God said to Abraham, "As for Sarai your wife, you shall not call her name Sarai, but Sarah shall be her name. 16I will bless her, and indeed I will give you a son by her. Then I will bless her, and she shall be a mother of nations; kings of peoples will come from her." 17Then Abraham fell on his face and laughed, and said in his heart, "Will a child be born to a man one hundred years old? And will Sarah, who is ninety years old, bear a child?" 18And Abraham said to God, "Oh that Ishmael might live before You!" 19But God said, "No, but Sarah your wife will bear you a son, and you shall call his name Isaac; and I will establish My covenant with him for an everlasting covenant for his descendants after him. 20As for Ishmael, I have heard you; behold, I will bless him, and will make him fruitful and will multiply him exceedingly. He shall become the father of twelve princes, and I will make him a great nation. 21But My covenant I will establish with Isaac, whom Sarah will bear to you at this season next year." 22When He finished talking with him, God went up from Abraham.

Notes and Discussion:

Observations:

Read   What does it say?

Reflect   What does it mean?

Respond   How does it apply?

Who is Isaac?
Genesis 21:1–20, NASB

Isaac Is Born

[1]Then the LORD took note of Sarah as He had said, and the LORD did for Sarah as He had promised. [2]So Sarah conceived and bore a son to Abraham in his old age, at the appointed time of which God had spoken to him.

[3]Abraham called the name of his son who was born to him, whom Sarah bore to him, Isaac. [4]Then Abraham circumcised his son Isaac when he was eight days old, as God had commanded him. [5]Now Abraham was one hundred years old when his son Isaac was born to him. [6]Sarah said, "God has made laughter for me; everyone who hears will laugh with me." [7]And she said, "Who would have said to Abraham that Sarah would nurse children? Yet I have borne him a son in his old age."

[8]The child grew and was weaned, and Abraham made a great feast on the day that Isaac was weaned.

[9]Now Sarah saw the son of Hagar the Egyptian, whom she had borne to Abraham, mocking.

[10]Therefore she said to Abraham, "Drive out this maid and her son, for the son of this maid shall not be an heir with my son Isaac."

[11]The matter distressed Abraham greatly because of his son.

[12]But God said to Abraham, "Do not be distressed because of the lad and your maid; whatever Sarah tells you, listen to her, for through Isaac your descendants shall be named. [13]And of the son of the maid I will make a nation also, because he is your descendant."

[14]So Abraham rose early in the morning and took bread and a skin of water and gave them to Hagar, putting them on her shoulder, and gave her the boy, and sent her away. And she departed and wandered about in the wilderness of Beersheba.

[15]When the water in the skin was used up, she left the boy under one of the bushes. [16]Then she went and sat down opposite him, about a bowshot away, for she said, "Do not let me see the boy die." And she sat opposite him, and lifted up her voice and wept.

[17]God heard the lad crying; and the angel of God called to Hagar from heaven and said to her, "What is the matter with you, Hagar? Do not fear, for God has heard the voice of the lad where he is. [18]Arise, lift up the lad, and hold him by the hand, for I will make a great nation of him."

[19]Then God opened her eyes and she saw a well of water; and she went and filled the skin with water and gave the lad a drink.

[20]God was with the lad, and he grew; and he lived in the wilderness and became an archer.

[21]He lived in the wilderness of Paran, and his mother took a wife for him from the land of Egypt.

Notes and Discussion:

Observations:

Read   What does it say?

Reflect   What does it mean?

Respond   How does it apply?

What happened on Mount Moriah?
What was the purpose of God's request?
Genesis 22:1–10, NASB

[1]Now it came about after these things, that God tested Abraham, and said to him, "Abraham!" And he said, "Here I am."

[2]He said, "Take now your son, your only son, whom you love, Isaac, and go to the land of Moriah, and offer him there as a burnt offering on one of the mountains of which I will tell you."

[3]So Abraham rose early in the morning and saddled his donkey, and took two of his young men with him and Isaac his son; and he split wood for the burnt offering, and arose and went to the place of which God had told him.

[4]On the third day Abraham raised his eyes and saw the place from a distance. [5]Abraham said to his young men, "Stay here with the donkey, and I and the lad will go over there; and we will worship and return to you."

[6]Abraham took the wood of the burnt offering and laid it on Isaac his son, and he took in his hand the fire and the knife. So the two of them walked on together. [7]Isaac spoke to Abraham his father and said, "My father!" And he said, "Here I am, my son." And he said, "Behold, the fire and the wood, but where is the lamb for the burnt offering?"

[8]Abraham said, "God will provide for Himself the lamb for the burnt offering, my son." So the two of them walked on together.

[9]Then they came to the place of which God had told him; and Abraham built the altar there and arranged the wood, and bound his son Isaac and laid him on the altar, on top of the wood. [10]Abraham stretched out his hand and took the knife to slay his son.

Observations:

What does it say?

What does it mean?

How does it apply?

Notes and Discussion:

What happened on Mount Moriah?
What was the purpose of God's request?
Genesis 22:11–18, NASB

¹¹But the angel of the LORD called to him from heaven and said, "Abraham, Abraham!" And he said, "Here I am."

¹²He said, "Do not stretch out your hand against the lad, and do nothing to him; for now I know that you fear God, since you have not withheld your son, your only son, from Me."

¹³Then Abraham raised his eyes and looked, and behold, behind him a ram caught in the thicket by his horns; and Abraham went and took the ram and offered him up for a burnt offering in the place of his son.

¹⁴Abraham called the name of that place The LORD Will Provide, as it is said to this day, "In the mount of the LORD it will be provided."

¹⁵Then the angel of the LORD called to Abraham a second time from heaven,

¹⁶and said, "By Myself I have sworn, declares the LORD, because you have done this thing and have not withheld your son, your only son,

¹⁷indeed I will greatly bless you, and I will greatly multiply your seed as the stars of the heavens and as the sand which is on the seashore; and your seed shall possess the gate of their enemies.

¹⁸In your seed all the nations of the earth shall be blessed, because you have obeyed My voice."

Observations:

What does it say?

What does it mean?

How does it apply?

Notes and Discussion:

Who is Jacob?
What can we learn about the sovereignty and grace of God?
Genesis 46:1-7, NASB

[1]So Israel set out with all that he had, and came to Beersheba, and offered sacrifices to the God of his father Isaac.

[2]God spoke to Israel in visions of the night and said, "Jacob, Jacob." And he said, "Here I am." [3]He said, "I am God, the God of your father; do not be afraid to go down to Egypt, for I will make you a great nation there.

[4]I will go down with you to Egypt, and I will also surely bring you up again; and Joseph will close your eyes."

[5]Then Jacob arose from Beersheba; and the sons of Israel carried their father Jacob and their little ones and their wives in the wagons which Pharaoh had sent to carry him.

[6]They took their livestock and their property, which they had acquired in the land of Canaan, and came to Egypt, Jacob and all his descendants with him:

[7]his sons and his grandsons with him, his daughters and his granddaughters, and all his descendants he brought with him to Egypt.

Observations:

Read   What does it say?

Reflect   What does it mean?

Respond   How does it apply?

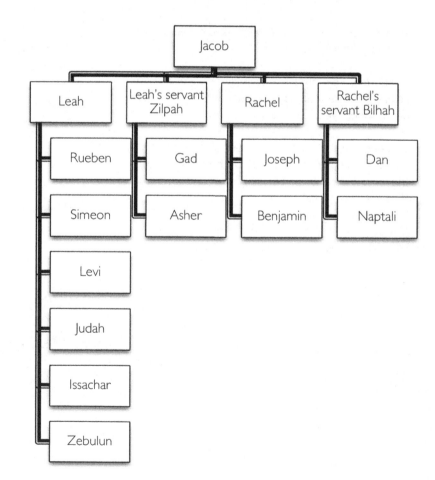

Notes and Discussion:

67

How did God use Israel's time in Egypt to advance His mission?
What can we learn about God's sovereignty?
Exodus 1:5–22, NASB

[5]All the persons who came from the loins of Jacob were seventy in number, but Joseph was already in Egypt. [6]Joseph died, and all his brothers and all that generation. [7]But the sons of Israel were fruitful and increased greatly, and multiplied, and became exceedingly mighty, so that the land was filled with them.

[8]Now a new king arose over Egypt, who did not know Joseph. [9]He said to his people, "Behold, the people of the sons of Israel are more and mightier than we. [10]Come, let us deal wisely with them, or else they will multiply and in the event of war, they will also join themselves to those who hate us, and fight against us and depart from the land."

[11]So they appointed taskmasters over them to afflict them with hard labor. And they built for Pharaoh storage cities, Pithom and Raamses.

[12]But the more they afflicted them, the more they multiplied and the more they spread out, so that they were in dread of the sons of Israel. [13]The Egyptians compelled the sons of Israel to labor rigorously; [14]and they made their lives bitter with hard labor in mortar and bricks and at all kinds of labor in the field, all their labors which they rigorously imposed on them.

[15]Then the king of Egypt spoke to the Hebrew midwives, one of whom was named Shiphrah and the other was named Puah; [16]and he said, "When you are helping the Hebrew women to give birth and see them upon the birthstool, if it is a son, then you shall put him to death; but if it is a daughter, then she shall live."

[17]But the midwives feared God, and did not do as the king of Egypt had commanded them, but let the boys live.

[18]So the king of Egypt called for the midwives and said to them, "Why have you done this thing, and let the boys live?" [19]The midwives said to Pharaoh, "Because the Hebrew women are not as the Egyptian women; for they are vigorous and give birth before the midwife can get to them."

[20]So God was good to the midwives, and the people multiplied, and became very mighty.

[21]Because the midwives feared God, He established households for them.

[22]Then Pharaoh commanded all his people, saying, "Every son who is born you are to cast into the Nile, and every daughter you are to keep alive."

Observations:

What does it say?

What does it mean?

How does it apply?

Notes and Discussion:

Who is Moses?
How does God work in the life of individuals to prepare them for God's mission?
Exodus 2:1–25, NASB

The Birth of Moses

¹Now a man from the house of Levi went and married a daughter of Levi. ²The woman conceived and bore a son; and when she saw that he was beautiful, she hid him for three months. ³But when she could hide him no longer, she got him a wicker basket and covered it over with tar and pitch. Then she put the child into it and set it among the reeds by the bank of the Nile. ⁴His sister stood at a distance to find out what would happen to him.

⁵The daughter of Pharaoh came down to bathe at the Nile, with her maidens walking alongside the Nile; and she saw the basket among the reeds and sent her maid, and she brought it to her. ⁶When she opened it, she saw the child, and behold, the boy was crying. And she had pity on him and said, "This is one of the Hebrews' children." ⁷Then his sister said to Pharaoh's daughter, "Shall I go and call a nurse for you from the Hebrew women that she may nurse the child for you?"

⁸Pharaoh's daughter said to her, "Go ahead." So the girl went and called the child's mother. ⁹Then Pharaoh's daughter said to her, "Take this child away and nurse him for me and I will give you your wages." So the woman took the child and nursed him.

¹⁰The child grew, and she brought him to Pharaoh's daughter and he became her son. And she named him Moses, and said, "Because I drew him out of the water."

¹¹Now it came about in those days, when Moses had grown up, that he went out to his brethren and looked on their hard labors; and he saw an Egyptian beating a Hebrew, one of his brethren.

¹²So he looked this way and that, and when he saw there was no one around, he struck down the Egyptian and hid him in the sand. ¹³He went out the next day, and behold, two Hebrews were fighting with each other; and he said to the offender, "Why are you striking your companion?"

¹⁴But he said, "Who made you a prince or a judge over us? Are you intending to kill me as you killed the Egyptian?" Then Moses was afraid and said, "Surely the matter has become known."

¹⁵When Pharaoh heard of this matter, he tried to kill Moses. But Moses fled from the presence of Pharaoh and settled in the land of Midian, and he sat down by a well.

²³Now it came about in the course of those many days that the king of Egypt died. And the sons of Israel sighed because of the bondage, and they cried out; and their cry for help because of their bondage rose up to God.

²⁴So God heard their groaning; and God remembered His covenant with Abraham, Isaac, and Jacob.

²⁵God saw the sons of Israel, and God took notice of them.

Who is Moses?
How does God work in the life of individuals to prepare them for God's mission?
Exodus 3:1–9, NASB

¹Now Moses was pasturing the flock of Jethro his father-in-law, the priest of Midian; and he led the flock to the west side of the wilderness and came to Horeb, the mountain of God.

²The angel of the LORD appeared to him in a blazing fire from the midst of a bush; and he looked, and behold, the bush was burning with fire, yet the bush was not consumed. ³So Moses said, "I must turn aside now and see this marvelous sight, why the bush is not burned up."

⁴When the LORD saw that he turned aside to look, God called to him from the midst of the bush and said, "Moses, Moses!" And he said, "Here I am." ⁵Then He said, "Do not come near here; remove your sandals from your feet, for the place on which you are standing is holy ground."

⁶He said also, "I am the God of your father, the God of Abraham, the God of Isaac, and the God of Jacob." Then Moses hid his face, for he was afraid to look at God.

⁷The LORD said, "I have surely seen the affliction of My people who are in Egypt, and have given heed to their cry because of their taskmasters, for I am aware of their sufferings.

⁸So I have come down to deliver them from the power of the Egyptians, and to bring them up from that land to a good and spacious land, to a land flowing with milk and honey, to the place of the Canaanite and the Hittite and the Amorite and the Perizzite and the Hivite and the Jebusite.

⁹Now, behold, the cry of the sons of Israel has come to Me; furthermore, I have seen the oppression with which the Egyptians are oppressing them.

Observations:

What does it say?

What does it mean?

How does it apply?

Notes and Discussion:

Who is Moses?
Exodus 3:10–22, NASB

The Mission of Moses

[10]Therefore, come now, and I will send you to Pharaoh, so that you may bring My people, the sons of Israel, out of Egypt." [11]But Moses said to God, "Who am I, that I should go to Pharaoh, and that I should bring the sons of Israel out of Egypt?" [12]And He said, "Certainly I will be with you, and this shall be the sign to you that it is I who have sent you: when you have brought the people out of Egypt, you shall worship God at this mountain."

[13]Then Moses said to God, "Behold, I am going to the sons of Israel, and I will say to them, 'The God of your fathers has sent me to you.' Now they may say to me, 'What is His name?' What shall I say to them?" [14]God said to Moses, "I AM WHO I AM"; and He said, "Thus you shall say to the sons of Israel, 'I AM has sent me to you.'" [15]God, furthermore, said to Moses, "Thus you shall say to the sons of Israel, 'The LORD, the God of your fathers, the God of Abraham, the God of Isaac, and the God of Jacob, has sent me to you.' This is My name forever, and this is My memorial-name to all generations.

[16]Go and gather the elders of Israel together and say to them, 'The LORD, the God of your fathers, the God of Abraham, Isaac and Jacob, has appeared to me, saying, "I am indeed concerned about you and what has been done to you in Egypt. [17]So I said, I will bring you up out of the affliction of Egypt to the land of the Canaanite and the Hittite and the Amorite and the Perizzite and the Hivite and the Jebusite, to a land flowing with milk and honey.'"

[18]They will pay heed to what you say; and you with the elders of Israel will come to the king of Egypt and you will say to him, 'The LORD, the God of the Hebrews, has met with us. So now, please, let us go a three days' journey into the wilderness, that we may sacrifice to the LORD our God.'

[19]But I know that the king of Egypt will not permit you to go, except under compulsion. [20]So I will stretch out My hand and strike Egypt with all My miracles which I shall do in the midst of it; and after that he will let you go. [21]I will grant this people favor in the sight of the Egyptians; and it shall be that when you go, you will not go empty-handed.

[22]But every woman shall ask of her neighbor and the woman who lives in her house, articles of silver and articles of gold, and clothing; and you will put them on your sons and daughters. Thus you will plunder the Egyptians."

Observations:

What does it say?

What does it mean?

How does it apply?

Notes and Discussion:

Observations:

Read   What does it say?

Reflect   What does it mean?

Respond   How does it apply?

Review
What am I learning?
Genesis, Exodus

Moses to David

Foundations of Faith

INVITED TO BELIEVE

Unit Essential Questions

1. How does God reveal and accomplish His mission from the time of Moses to David?

2. How does understanding the progression of God's plan from Moses to David impact my life?

Unit Learning Objectives

A. To understand how God continues to advance His mission to reflect His glory by turning a multitude into a nation

B. To practice the skills of inductive Bible study and exegetical conversations within community

Unit Learning Assessments

1. Formative Quizzes

2. Summative Assessment

Daily Essential Questions

1. What is the Passover?

2. How did God turn a multitude into a nation?

3. What happened on Mount Sinai?

4. What is the tabernacle?

5. What is the Day of Atonement?

6. Who is Joshua?

7. How does God use the Jordan River and Jericho to reveal His glory?

8. Who is Rahab?

9. Who is Ruth?

10. Who is Saul?

11. Review: What am I learning?

12. Assessment: How will I demonstrate what I have learned?

Moses to David

God designates and trains a leader for His people and prepares to deliver the multitude from their bondage in Egypt, but His mission is not yet complete.

Over the previous 400 years, God's people have begun to identify with the customs of the Egyptians and their culture of bondage. In addition to freeing the people physically from their slavery, God must renew their minds. He must "work the Egypt out of them" before they can enter into their new land.

In some ways, what happens next is a lot like the New Covenant process of justification, sanctification, and glorification.

Justification is what happens at the moment of salvation. When you or I accept the gift of God's payment of sin through the life, death, and resurrection of Christ, we are forgiven of our sins and immediately released from the bondage of our sin. Sanctification is the process that occurs next. It is the time that God trains us to respond to His invitations, to renew our minds, and to reflect Him with every aspect of our life. Glorification is what happens after death, when we enter into the presence of God to spend eternity with Him in our glorified and perfected bodies.

Similarly, after the Passover, the people of God are physically delivered from their bondage and slavery in Egypt, but instead of leading them directly to the Promised Land, God takes the long route out of Egypt to retrain them to follow Him.

In order to change them from a mob to a people who live out God's mission to reflect His glory to the earth, God will bring them to a mountain and create a new culture through new commandments.

This new law will set them distinctly apart from every other culture on the face of the earth.

God will give them a new way of life and a new way to live. After a major failure and 40 years of retraining, He will raise up a new leader and finally bring them to the Land of Promise.

However, instead of faithfully following and living out their purpose in the land, the people will again rebel, asking for a human king so that they can become like those around them.

God will appoint the prophet Samuel, and then eventually He will appoint a shepherd to lead His people. It is through the shepherd who becomes king that Jerusalem, the city of God, will be established, and the nation of Israel will have an archetype of the prophet, priest, and king, that will later be fulfilled through Jesus Christ.

What is the Passover?
How does the way that God delivers Israel from Egypt reflect His glory?
Exodus 12:1–20, NASB

¹Now the LORD said to Moses and Aaron in the land of Egypt, ²"This month shall be the beginning of months for you; it is to be the first month of the year to you. ³Speak to all the congregation of Israel, saying, 'On the tenth of this month they are each one to take a lamb for themselves, according to their fathers' households, a lamb for each household.

⁴Now if the household is too small for a lamb, then he and his neighbor nearest to his house are to take one according to the number of persons in them; according to what each man should eat, you are to divide the lamb.

⁵Your lamb shall be an unblemished male a year old; you may take it from the sheep or from the goats. ⁶You shall keep it until the fourteenth day of the same month, then the whole assembly of the congregation of Israel is to kill it at twilight.

⁷Moreover, they shall take some of the blood and put it on the two doorposts and on the lintel of the houses in which they eat it. ⁸They shall eat the flesh that same night, roasted with fire, and they shall eat it with unleavened bread and bitter herbs.

⁹Do not eat any of it raw or boiled at all with water, but rather roasted with fire, both its head and its legs along with its entrails. ¹⁰And you shall not leave any of it over until morning, but whatever is left of it until morning, you shall burn with fire.

¹¹Now you shall eat it in this manner: with your loins girded, your sandals on your feet, and your staff in your hand; and you shall eat it in haste—it is the LORD's Passover.

¹²For I will go through the land of Egypt on that night, and will strike down all the firstborn in the land of Egypt, both man and beast; and against all the gods of Egypt I will execute judgments—I am the LORD. ¹³The blood shall be a sign for you on the houses where you live; and when I see the blood I will pass over you, and no plague will befall you to destroy you when I strike the land of Egypt.

¹⁴"Now this day will be a memorial to you, and you shall celebrate it as a feast to the LORD; throughout your generations you are to celebrate it as a permanent ordinance.

¹⁵Seven days you shall eat unleavened bread, but on the first day you shall remove leaven from your houses; for whoever eats anything leavened from the first day until the seventh day, that person shall be cut off from Israel. ¹⁶On the first day you shall have a holy assembly, and another holy assembly on the seventh day; no work at all shall be done on them, except what must be eaten by every person, that alone may be prepared by you.

¹⁷You shall also observe the Feast of Unleavened Bread, for on this very day I brought your hosts out of the land of Egypt; therefore you shall observe this day throughout your generations as a permanent ordinance. ¹⁸In the first month, on the fourteenth day of the month at evening, you shall eat unleavened bread, until the twenty-first day of the month at evening.

¹⁹Seven days there shall be no leaven found in your houses; for whoever eats what is leavened, that person shall be cut off from the congregation of Israel, whether he is an alien or a native of the land. ²⁰You shall not eat anything leavened; in all your dwellings you shall eat unleavened bread.'"

What is the Passover?
Exodus 12:21–30, NASB

21Then Moses called for all the elders of Israel and said to them, "Go and take for yourselves lambs according to your families, and slay the Passover lamb. 22You shall take a bunch of hyssop and dip it in the blood which is in the basin, and apply some of the blood that is in the basin to the lintel and the two doorposts; and none of you shall go outside the door of his house until morning.

23For the LORD will pass through to smite the Egyptians; and when He sees the blood on the lintel and on the two doorposts, the LORD will pass over the door and will not allow the destroyer to come in to your houses to smite you. 24And you shall observe this event as an ordinance for you and your children forever. 25When you enter the land which the LORD will give you, as He has promised, you shall observe this rite. 26And when your children say to you, 'What does this rite mean to you?' 27you shall say, 'It is a Passover sacrifice to the LORD who passed over the houses of the sons of Israel in Egypt when He smote the Egyptians, but spared our homes.'" And the people bowed low and worshiped.

28Then the sons of Israel went and did so; just as the LORD had commanded Moses and Aaron, so they did.

29Now it came about at midnight that the LORD struck all the firstborn in the land of Egypt, from the firstborn of Pharaoh who sat on his throne to the firstborn of the captive who was in the dungeon, and all the firstborn of cattle. 30Pharaoh arose in the night, he and all his servants and all the Egyptians, and there was a great cry in Egypt, for there was no home where there was not someone dead.

Observations:

What does it say?

What does it mean?

How does it apply?

Notes and Discussion:

What is the Passover?
How does the way that God delivers Israel from Egypt reflect His glory?
Exodus 12:31–42, NASB

³¹Then he called for Moses and Aaron at night and said, "Rise up, get out from among my people, both you and the sons of Israel; and go, worship the LORD, as you have said. ³²Take both your flocks and your herds, as you have said, and go, and bless me also."

³³The Egyptians urged the people, to send them out of the land in haste, for they said, "We will all be dead." ³⁴So the people took their dough before it was leavened, with their kneading bowls bound up in the clothes on their shoulders.

³⁵Now the sons of Israel had done according to the word of Moses, for they had requested from the Egyptians articles of silver and articles of gold, and clothing; ³⁶and the LORD had given the people favor in the sight of the Egyptians, so that they let them have their request. Thus they plundered the Egyptians.

³⁷Now the sons of Israel journeyed from Rameses to Succoth, about six hundred thousand men on foot, aside from children. ³⁸A mixed multitude also went up with them, along with flocks and herds, a very large number of livestock.

³⁹They baked the dough which they had brought out of Egypt into cakes of unleavened bread. For it had not become leavened, since they were driven out of Egypt and could not delay, nor had they prepared any provisions for themselves.

⁴⁰Now the time that the sons of Israel lived in Egypt was four hundred and thirty years. ⁴¹And at the end of four hundred and thirty years, to the very day, all the hosts of the LORD went out from the land of Egypt.

Ordinance of the Passover

⁴²It is a night to be observed for the LORD for having brought them out from the land of Egypt; this night is for the LORD, to be observed by all the sons of Israel throughout their generations.

Observations:

What does it say?

What does it mean?

How does it apply?

Notes and Discussion:

God provides through _____ and _____ .

Definition of *atonement*:

Definition of *forbearance*:

How did God turn a multitude into a nation?
How did God "work the Egypt out" of the people?
Exodus 13:17–22, NASB

Notes and Discussion:

[17]Now when Pharaoh had let the people go, God did not lead them by the way of the land of the Philistines, even though it was near; for God said, "The people might change their minds when they see war, and return to Egypt."

[18]Hence God led the people around by the way of the wilderness to the Red Sea; and the sons of Israel went up in martial array from the land of Egypt.

[19]Moses took the bones of Joseph with him, for he had made the sons of Israel solemnly swear, saying, "God will surely take care of you, and you shall carry my bones from here with you."

[20]Then they set out from Succoth and camped in Etham on the edge of the wilderness.

[21]The Lord was going before them in a pillar of cloud by day to lead them on the way, and in a pillar of fire by night to give them light, that they might travel by day and by night.

[22]He did not take away the pillar of cloud by day, nor the pillar of fire by night, from before the people.

How did God turn a multitude into a nation?
How did God "work the Egypt out" of the people?
Exodus 14:1–11, NASB

Notes and Discussion:

[1]Now the LORD spoke to Moses, saying, [2]"Tell the sons of Israel to turn back and camp before Pi-hahiroth, between Migdol and the sea; you shall camp in front of Baal-zephon, opposite it, by the sea.

[3]For Pharaoh will say of the sons of Israel, 'They are wandering aimlessly in the land; the wilderness has shut them in.' [4]Thus I will harden Pharaoh's heart, and he will chase after them; and I will be honored through Pharaoh and all his army, and the Egyptians will know that I am the LORD." And they did so.

[5]When the king of Egypt was told that the people had fled, Pharaoh and his servants had a change of heart toward the people, and they said, "What is this we have done, that we have let Israel go from serving us?"

[6]So he made his chariot ready and took his people with him; [7]and he took six hundred select chariots, and all the other chariots of Egypt with officers over all of them.

[8]The LORD hardened the heart of Pharaoh, king of Egypt, and he chased after the sons of Israel as the sons of Israel were going out boldly.

[9]Then the Egyptians chased after them with all the horses and chariots of Pharaoh, his horsemen and his army, and they overtook them camping by the sea, beside Pi-hahiroth, in front of Baal-zephon.

[10]As Pharaoh drew near, the sons of Israel looked, and behold, the Egyptians were marching after them, and they became very frightened; so the sons of Israel cried out to the LORD. [11]Then they said to Moses, "Is it because there were no graves in Egypt that you have taken us away to die in the wilderness? Why have you dealt with us in this way, bringing us out of Egypt?

How did God turn a multitude into a nation?
Exodus 14:12–21, NASB

[12]Is this not the word that we spoke to you in Egypt, saying, "Leave us alone that we may serve the Egyptians"? For it would have been better for us to serve the Egyptians than to die in the wilderness.

[13]But Moses said to the people, "Do not fear! Stand by and see the salvation of the LORD which He will accomplish for you today; for the Egyptians whom you have seen today, you will never see them again forever. [14]The LORD will fight for you while you keep silent."

[15]Then the LORD said to Moses, "Why are you crying out to Me? Tell the sons of Israel to go forward. [16]As for you, lift up your staff and stretch out your hand over the sea and divide it, and the sons of Israel shall go through the midst of the sea on dry land. [17]As for Me, behold, I will harden the hearts of the Egyptians so that they will go in after them; and I will be honored through Pharaoh and all his army, through his chariots and his horsemen. [18]Then the Egyptians will know that I am the LORD, when I am honored through Pharaoh, through his chariots and his horsemen."

[19]The angel of God, who had been going before the camp of Israel, moved and went behind them; and the pillar of cloud moved from before them and stood behind them. [20]So it came between the camp of Egypt and the camp of Israel; and there was the cloud along with the darkness, yet it gave light at night. Thus the one did not come near the other all night.

[21]Then Moses stretched out his hand over the sea; and the LORD swept the sea back by a strong east wind all night and turned the sea into dry land, so the waters were divided.

Observations:

What does it say?

What does it mean?

How does it apply?

Notes and Discussion:

How did God reveal Himself to a new generation?
Exodus 14:22–31, NASB

22The sons of Israel went through the midst of the sea on the dry land, and the waters were like a wall to them on their right hand and on their left.

23Then the Egyptians took up the pursuit, and all Pharaoh's horses, his chariots and his horsemen went in after them into the midst of the sea.

24At the morning watch, the LORD looked down on the army of the Egyptians through the pillar of fire and cloud and brought the army of the Egyptians into confusion. 25He caused their chariot wheels to swerve, and He made them drive with difficulty; so the Egyptians said, "Let us flee from Israel, for the LORD is fighting for them against the Egyptians."

26Then the LORD said to Moses, "Stretch out your hand over the sea so that the waters may come back over the Egyptians, over their chariots and their horsemen."

27So Moses stretched out his hand over the sea, and the sea returned to its normal state at daybreak, while the Egyptians were fleeing right into it; then the LORD overthrew the Egyptians in the midst of the sea.

28The waters returned and covered the chariots and the horsemen, even Pharaoh's entire army that had gone into the sea after them; not even one of them remained.

29But the sons of Israel walked on dry land through the midst of the sea, and the waters were like a wall to them on their right hand and on their left.

30Thus the LORD saved Israel that day from the hand of the Egyptians, and Israel saw the Egyptians dead on the seashore.

31When Israel saw the great power which the LORD had used against the Egyptians, the people feared the LORD, and they believed in the LORD and in His servant Moses.

Notes and Discussion:

What happened on Mount Sinai?
Why did God give the people His commandments?
Exodus 19:1–12, NASB

[1]In the third month after the sons of Israel had gone out of the land of Egypt, on that very day they came into the wilderness of Sinai. [2]When they set out from Rephidim, they came to the wilderness of Sinai and camped in the wilderness; and there Israel camped in front of the mountain.

[3]Moses went up to God, and the LORD called to him from the mountain, saying, "Thus you shall say to the house of Jacob and tell the sons of Israel:

[4]'You yourselves have seen what I did to the Egyptians, and how I bore you on eagles' wings, and brought you to Myself. [5]Now then, if you will indeed obey My voice and keep My covenant, then you shall be My own possession among all the peoples, for all the earth is Mine; [6]and you shall be to Me a kingdom of priests and a holy nation.' These are the words that you shall speak to the sons of Israel."

[7]So Moses came and called the elders of the people, and set before them all these words which the LORD had commanded him. [8]All the people answered together and said, "All that the LORD has spoken we will do!" And Moses brought back the words of the people to the LORD.

[9]The LORD said to Moses, "Behold, I will come to you in a thick cloud, so that the people may hear when I speak with you and may also believe in you forever." Then Moses told the words of the people to the LORD.

[10]The LORD also said to Moses, "Go to the people and consecrate them today and tomorrow, and let them wash their garments; [11]and let them be ready for the third day, for on the third day the LORD will come down on Mount Sinai in the sight of all the people. [12]You shall set bounds for the people all around, saying, 'Beware that you do not go up on the mountain or touch the border of it; whoever touches the mountain shall surely be put to death.

Observations:

What does it say?

What does it mean?

How does it apply?

Notes and Discussion:

Exodus 19:16–25, NASB

16So it came about on the third day, when it was morning, that there were thunder and lightning flashes and a thick cloud upon the mountain and a very loud trumpet sound, so that all the people who were in the camp trembled. 17And Moses brought the people out of the camp to meet God, and they stood at the foot of the mountain.

18Now Mount Sinai was all in smoke because the LORD descended upon it in fire; and its smoke ascended like the smoke of a furnace, and the whole mountain quaked violently. 19When the sound of the trumpet grew louder and louder, Moses spoke and God answered him with thunder. 20The LORD came down on Mount Sinai, to the top of the mountain; and the LORD called Moses to the top of the mountain, and Moses went up.

21Then the LORD spoke to Moses, "Go down, warn the people, so that they do not break through to the LORD to gaze, and many of them perish.

22Also let the priests who come near to the LORD consecrate themselves, or else the LORD will break out against them." 23Moses said to the LORD, "The people cannot come up to Mount Sinai, for You warned us, saying, 'Set bounds about the mountain and consecrate it.'"

24Then the LORD said to him, "Go down and come up again, you and Aaron with you; but do not let the priests and the people break through to come up to the LORD, or He will break forth upon them."

25So Moses went down to the people and told them.

Observations:

Read   What does it say?

Reflect   What does it mean?

Respond   How does it apply?

Why did God give the people His commandments?
Exodus 20:1–17, NASB

Then God spoke all these words, saying,

2"I am the LORD your God, who brought you out of the land of Egypt, out of the house of slavery.
3"You shall have no other gods before Me.
4"You shall not make for yourself an idol, or any likeness of what is in heaven above or on the earth beneath or in the water under the earth.
5You shall not worship them or serve them; for I, the LORD your God, am a jealous God, visiting the iniquity of the fathers on the children, on the third and the fourth generations of those who hate Me,
6but showing loving kindness to thousands, to those who love Me and keep My commandments.
7"You shall not take the name of the LORD your God in vain, for the LORD will not leave him unpunished who takes His name in vain.
8"Remember the Sabbath day, to keep it holy. 9Six days you shall labor and do all your work, 10but the seventh day is a Sabbath of the LORD your God; in it you shall not do any work, you or your son or your daughter, your male or your female servant or your cattle or your sojourner who stays with you. 11For in six days the LORD made the heavens and the earth, the sea and all that is in them, and rested on the seventh day; therefore the LORD blessed the Sabbath day and made it holy.
12"Honor your father and your mother, that your days may be prolonged in the land which the LORD your God gives you.
13"You shall not murder.
14"You shall not commit adultery.
15"You shall not steal.
16"You shall not bear false witness against your neighbor.
17"You shall not covet your neighbor's house; you shall not covet your neighbor's wife or his male servant or his female servant or his ox or his donkey or anything that belongs to your neighbor."

Observations:

What does it say?

What does it mean?

How does it apply?

Notes and Discussion:

God provides the law

- The law was given by God to Moses for the _____ _____ _____ _____.

  Exodus 24:12

- The law is a _____ to the _____ of the hearts of God's people.

  Deuteronomy 31:26–27

- The law is to be _____

  the promise that it will bring _____.

  Joshua 1:8

- Following the law brings blessing. Ignoring the law brings cursing.

  Deuteronomy 7

Summarize the following verses.

- Joshua 8:34

- 1 Kings 2:3

- Daniel 9:13

- Hosea 4:6

- Amos 2:4

- Malachi 2:9

God provides the law

- Sin was in the world prior to_____ _____ _____ _____.

  Romans 5:13

- It is through the law that we become _____ of _____ _____ and our _____ _____ _____.

  Romans 3:20

- The law was given so that we would become aware of our sin and our need for _____.

  Romans 5:20

- The law does not lead to _____ and a right relationship with God because it is not based on _____ _____ _____ but on _____ _____ _____ _____ _____.

  Galatians 3:11–12

Application: What role does the law play in the mission of God?

Exodus 32:1–8, NASB

¹Now when the people saw that Moses delayed to come down from the mountain, the people assembled about Aaron and said to him, "Come, make us a god who will go before us; as for this Moses, the man who brought us up from the land of Egypt, we do not know what has become of him." ²Aaron said to them, "Tear off the gold rings which are in the ears of your wives, your sons, and your daughters, and bring them to me." ³Then all the people tore off the gold rings which were in their ears and brought them to Aaron. ⁴He took this from their hand, and fashioned it with a graving tool and made it into a molten calf; and they said, "This is your god, O Israel, who brought you up from the land of Egypt."

⁵Now when Aaron saw this, he built an altar before it; and Aaron made a proclamation and said, "Tomorrow shall be a feast to the LORD." ⁶So the next day they rose early and offered burnt offerings, and brought peace offerings; and the people sat down to eat and to drink, and rose up to play.

⁷Then the LORD spoke to Moses, "Go down at once, for your people, whom you brought up from the land of Egypt, have corrupted themselves. ⁸They have quickly turned aside from the way which I commanded them. They have made for themselves a molten calf, and have worshiped it and have sacrificed to it and said, 'This is your god, O Israel, who brought you up from the land of Egypt!'"

Observations:

Read   What does it say?

Reflect   What does it mean?

Respond   How does it apply?

How did God's people respond to His commands?
Exodus 32:19–28, NASB

¹⁹It came about, as soon as Moses came near the camp, that he saw the calf and the dancing; and Moses' anger burned, and he threw the tablets from his hands and shattered them at the foot of the mountain. ²⁰He took the calf which they had made and burned it with fire, and ground it to powder, and scattered it over the surface of the water and made the sons of Israel drink it.

²¹Then Moses said to Aaron, "What did this people do to you, that you have brought such great sin upon them?"

²²Aaron said, "Do not let the anger of my lord burn; you know the people yourself, that they are prone to evil. ²³For they said to me, 'Make a god for us who will go before us; for this Moses, the man who brought us up from the land of Egypt, we do not know what has become of him.'

²⁴I said to them, 'Whoever has any gold, let them tear it off.' So they gave it to me, and I threw it into the fire, and out came this calf."

²⁵Now when Moses saw that the people were out of control—for Aaron had let them get out of control to be a derision among their enemies—²⁶then Moses stood in the gate of the camp, and said, "Whoever is for the LORD, come to me!" And all the sons of Levi gathered together to him.

²⁷He said to them, "Thus says the LORD, the God of Israel, 'Every man of you put his sword upon his thigh, and go back and forth from gate to gate in the camp, and kill every man his brother, and every man his friend, and every man his neighbor.'"

²⁸So the sons of Levi did as Moses instructed, and about three thousand men of the people fell that day.

Observations:

What does it say?

What does it mean?

How does it apply?

Notes and Discussion:

Notes and Discussion:

Reflection and Application:

God's conditions for His people
How do I understand what happens next?

Deuteronomy 8

The promise of blessing

[1]"All the commandments that I am commanding you today you shall be careful to do, that you may live and multiply, and go in and possess the land which the LORD swore to give to your forefathers. [2]You shall remember all the way which the LORD your God has led you in the wilderness these forty years, that He might humble you, testing you, to know what was in your heart, whether you would keep His commandments or not. [3]He humbled you and let you be hungry, and fed you with manna which you did not know, nor did your fathers know, that He might make you understand that man does not live by bread alone, but man lives by everything that proceeds out of the mouth of the LORD. [4]Your clothing did not wear out on you, nor did your foot swell these forty years.

[5]Thus you are to know in your heart that the LORD your God was disciplining you just as a man disciplines his son.

[6]Therefore, you shall keep the commandments of the LORD your God, to walk in His ways and to fear Him. [7]For the LORD your God is bringing you into a good land, a land of brooks of water, of fountains and springs, flowing forth in valleys and hills; [8]a land of wheat and barley, of vines and fig trees and pomegranates, a land of olive oil and honey; [9]a land where you will eat food without scarcity, in which you will not lack anything; a land whose stones are iron, and out of whose hills you can dig copper. [10]When you have eaten and are satisfied, you shall bless the LORD your God for the good land which He has given you.

[11]"Beware that you do not forget the LORD your God by not keeping His commandments and His ordinances and His statutes which I am commanding you today;

[12]otherwise, when you have eaten and are satisfied, and have built good houses and lived in them, [13]and when your herds and your flocks multiply, and your silver and gold multiply, and all that you have multiplies, [14]then your heart will become proud and you will forget the LORD your God who brought you out from the land of Egypt, out of the house of slavery. [15]He led you through the great and terrible wilderness, with its fiery serpents and scorpions and thirsty ground where there was no water; He brought water for you out of the rock of flint. [16]In the wilderness He fed you manna which your fathers did not know, that He might humble you and that He might test you, to do good for you in the end.

[17]Otherwise, you may say in your heart, 'My power and the strength of my hand made me this wealth.' [18]But you shall remember the LORD your God, for it is He who is giving you power to make wealth, that He may confirm His covenant which He swore to your fathers, as it is this day. [19]It shall come about if you ever forget the LORD your God and go after other gods and serve them and worship them, I testify against you today that you will surely perish. [20]Like the nations that the LORD makes to perish before you, so you shall perish; because you would not listen to the voice of the LORD your God.

The promise of blessing and curses

Obedience brings:		Disobedience brings:
Blessings in the city and the country		Curses in the city and the country
Many children		Barren and infertile
Plentiful crops		Destroyed crops
Fertile livestock		Infertile livestock
Abundance of bread and grain		Scarce bread and grain
Blessings coming and going		Curses coming and going
Enemies defeated		Enemies victorious
Being established as the people of God		Being ridiculed by other nations
Being feared by other nations		Being filled with fear and despair
Plentiful rain		Powder and dust instead of rain
Other nations will be in debt to Israel		Being in debt to other nations
Being the head and not the tail		Being the tail and not the head
		Being afflicted with disease

Significance and application:

1.   How does this advance the mission of God?

2.   How does this help us understand the narrative of the rest of the Old Testament?

3.   How does this help us understand the reception of Christ by the Jews?

What is the tabernacle?
How did God reveal Himself to His people in the wilderness?
Exodus 39:32–43, 40:1–8, NASB

32Thus all the work of the tabernacle of the tent of meeting was completed; and the sons of Israel did according to all that the LORD had commanded Moses; so they did.

33They brought the tabernacle to Moses, the tent and all its furnishings: its clasps, its boards, its bars, and its pillars and its sockets; 34and the covering of rams' skins dyed red, and the covering of porpoise skins, and the screening veil; 35the ark of the testimony and its poles and the mercy seat; 36the table, all its utensils, and the bread of the Presence; 37the pure gold lampstand, with its arrangement of lamps and all its utensils, and the oil for the light; 38and the gold altar, and the anointing oil and the fragrant incense, and the veil for the doorway of the tent; 39the bronze altar and its bronze grating, its poles and all its utensils, the laver and its stand; 40the hangings for the court, its pillars and its sockets, and the screen for the gate of the court, its cords and its pegs and all the equipment for the service of the tabernacle, for the tent of meeting; 41the woven garments for ministering in the holy place and the holy garments for Aaron the priest and the garments of his sons, to minister as priests.

42So the sons of Israel did all the work according to all that the LORD had commanded Moses.

43And Moses examined all the work and behold, they had done it; just as the LORD had commanded, this they had done. So Moses blessed them.

Exodus 39:32–43, NASB

1Then the LORD spoke to Moses, saying, 2"On the first day of the first month you shall set up the tabernacle of the tent of meeting.

3You shall place the ark of the testimony there, and you shall screen the ark with the veil. 4You shall bring in the table and arrange what belongs on it; and you shall bring in the lampstand and mount its lamps. 5Moreover, you shall set the gold altar of incense before the ark of the testimony, and set up the veil for the doorway to the tabernacle. 6You shall set the altar of burnt offering in front of the doorway of the tabernacle of the tent of meeting. 7You shall set the laver between the tent of meeting and the altar and put water in it. 8You shall set up the court all around and hang up the veil for the gateway of the court.

Exodus 40:1–8, NASB

Notes and Discussion:

Exodus 40:30–38, Numbers 9:15–18a, NASB

[20]Then he [Moses] took the testimony and put it into the ark, and attached the poles to the ark, and put the mercy seat on top of the ark. [21]He brought the ark into the tabernacle, and set up a veil for the screen, and screened off the ark of the testimony, just as the LORD had commanded Moses.

[22]Then he put the table in the tent of meeting on the north side of the tabernacle, outside the veil. [23]He set the arrangement of bread in order on it before the LORD, just as the LORD had commanded Moses.

[24]Then he placed the lampstand in the tent of meeting, opposite the table, on the south side of the tabernacle. [25]He lighted the lamps before the LORD, just as the LORD had commanded Moses. [26]Then he placed the gold altar in the tent of meeting in front of the veil; [27]and he burned fragrant incense on it, just as the LORD had commanded Moses.

[28]Then he set up the veil for the doorway of the tabernacle. [29]He set the altar of burnt offering before the doorway of the tabernacle of the tent of meeting, and offered on it the burnt offering and the meal offering, just as the LORD had commanded Moses. [30]He placed the laver between the tent of meeting and the altar and put water in it for washing.

[31]From it Moses and Aaron and his sons washed their hands and their feet.

[32]When they entered the tent of meeting, and when they approached the altar, they washed, just as the LORD had commanded Moses.

[33]He erected the court all around the tabernacle and the altar, and hung up the veil for the gateway of the court. Thus Moses finished the work.

[34]Then the cloud covered the tent of meeting, and the glory of the LORD filled the tabernacle. [35]Moses was not able to enter the tent of meeting because the cloud had settled on it, and the glory of the LORD filled the tabernacle.

[36]Throughout all their journeys whenever the cloud was taken up from over the tabernacle, the sons of Israel would set out; [37]but if the cloud was not taken up, then they did not set out until the day when it was taken up. [38]For throughout all their journeys, the cloud of the LORD was on the tabernacle by day, and there was fire in it by night, in the sight of all the house of Israel.

Exodus 40:20-38

[15]Now on the day that the tabernacle was erected the cloud covered the tabernacle, the tent of the testimony, and in the evening it was like the appearance of fire over the tabernacle, until morning. [16]So it was continuously; the cloud would cover it by day, and the appearance of fire by night. [17]Whenever the cloud was lifted from over the tent, afterward the sons of Israel would then set out; and in the place where the cloud settled down, there the sons of Israel would camp. [18]At the command of the LORD the sons of Israel would set out, and at the command of the LORD they would camp;

Numbers 9:15-18a

What is the Day of Atonement?
How did God continue to provide reconciliation for His people?
Leviticus 16:1–19, NASB

[1]Now the LORD spoke to Moses after the death of the two sons of Aaron, when they had approached the presence of the LORD and died.

[2]The LORD said to Moses: "Tell your brother Aaron that he shall not enter at any time into the holy place inside the veil, before the mercy seat which is on the ark, or he will die; for I will appear in the cloud over the mercy seat. [3]Aaron shall enter the holy place with this: with a bull for a sin offering and a ram for a burnt offering.

[4]He shall put on the holy linen tunic, and the linen undergarments shall be next to his body, and he shall be girded with the linen sash and attired with the linen turban (these are holy garments). Then he shall bathe his body in water and put them on. [5]He shall take from the congregation of the sons of Israel two male goats for a sin offering and one ram for a burnt offering.

[6]"Then Aaron shall offer the bull for the sin offering which is for himself, that he may make atonement for himself and for his household.

[7]He shall take the two goats and present them before the LORD at the doorway of the tent of meeting. [8]Aaron shall cast lots for the two goats, one lot for the LORD and the other lot for the scapegoat. [9]Then Aaron shall offer the goat on which the lot for the LORD fell, and make it a sin offering. [10]But the goat on which the lot for the scapegoat fell shall be presented alive before the LORD, to make atonement upon it, to send it into the wilderness as the scapegoat.

[11]"Then Aaron shall offer the bull of the sin offering which is for himself and make atonement for himself and for his household, and he shall slaughter the bull of the sin offering which is for himself.

[12]He shall take a firepan full of coals of fire from upon the altar before the LORD and two handfuls of finely ground sweet incense, and bring it inside the veil. [13]He shall put the incense on the fire before the LORD, that the cloud of incense may cover the mercy seat that is on the ark of the testimony, otherwise he will die. [14]Moreover, he shall take some of the blood of the bull and sprinkle it with his finger on the mercy seat on the east side; also in front of the mercy seat he shall sprinkle some of the blood with his finger seven times.

[15]"Then he shall slaughter the goat of the sin offering which is for the people, and bring its blood inside the veil and do with its blood as he did with the blood of the bull, and sprinkle it on the mercy seat and in front of the mercy seat. [16]He shall make atonement for the holy place, because of the impurities of the sons of Israel and because of their transgressions in regard to all their sins; and thus he shall do for the tent of meeting which abides with them in the midst of their impurities.

[17]When he goes in to make atonement in the holy place, no one shall be in the tent of meeting until he comes out, that he may make atonement for himself and for his household and for all the assembly of Israel. [18]Then he shall go out to the altar that is before the LORD and make atonement for it, and shall take some of the blood of the bull and of the blood of the goat and put it on the horns of the altar on all sides. [19]With his finger he shall sprinkle some of the blood on it seven times and cleanse it, and from the impurities of the sons of Israel consecrate it.

What is the Day of Atonement?
How did God continue to provide reconciliation for His people?
Leviticus 16:20–22, 29–34, NASB

20"When he finishes atoning for the holy place and the tent of meeting and the altar, he shall offer the live goat. 21Then Aaron shall lay both of his hands on the head of the live goat, and confess over it all the iniquities of the sons of Israel and all their transgressions in regard to all their sins; and he shall lay them on the head of the goat and send it away into the wilderness by the hand of a man who stands in readiness. 22The goat shall bear on itself all their iniquities to a solitary land; and he shall release the goat in the wilderness.

29"This shall be a permanent statute for you: in the seventh month, on the tenth day of the month, you shall humble your souls and not do any work, whether the native, or the alien who sojourns among you; 30for it is on this day that atonement shall be made for you to cleanse you; you will be clean from all your sins before the LORD.

31It is to be a sabbath of solemn rest for you, that you may humble your souls; it is a permanent statute.

32So the priest who is anointed and ordained to serve as priest in his father's place shall make atonement: he shall thus put on the linen garments, the holy garments, 33and make atonement for the holy sanctuary, and he shall make atonement for the tent of meeting and for the altar. He shall also make atonement for the priests and for all the people of the assembly. 34Now you shall have this as a permanent statute, to make atonement for the sons of Israel for all their sins once every year." And just as the LORD had commanded Moses, so he did.

- God provides through _____ and _____ .

  Definition of *atonement*:

  Definition of *forbearance*:

Additional key words and concepts:

Who is Joshua?
What happened when the Israelites failed to place their faith in God?
Numbers 13:1–3, 17–33, NASB

[1]Then the LORD spoke to Moses saying, [2]"Send out for yourself men so that they may spy out the land of Canaan, which I am going to give to the sons of Israel; you shall send a man from each of their fathers' tribes, every one a leader among them." [3]So Moses sent them from the wilderness of Paran at the command of the LORD, all of them men who were heads of the sons of Israel.

[17]When Moses sent them to spy out the land of Canaan, he said to them, "Go up there into the Negev; then go up into the hill country. [18] See what the land is like, and whether the people who live in it are strong or weak, whether they are few or many.

[19]How is the land in which they live, is it good or bad? And how are the cities in which they live, are they like open camps or with fortifications?

[20]How is the land, is it fat or lean? Are there trees in it or not? Make an effort then to get some of the fruit of the land." Now the time was the time of the first ripe grapes.

[21]So they went up and spied out the land from the wilderness of Zin as far as Rehob, at Lebo-hamath. [22]When they had gone up into the Negev, they came to Hebron where Ahiman, Sheshai and Talmai, the descendants of Anak were. (Now Hebron was built seven years before Zoan in Egypt.)

[23]Then they came to the valley of Eshcol and from there cut down a branch with a single cluster of grapes; and they carried it on a pole between two men, with some of the pomegranates and the figs. [24]That place was called the valley of Eshcol, because of the cluster which the sons of Israel cut down from there.

[25]When they returned from spying out the land, at the end of forty days, [26]they proceeded to come to Moses and Aaron and to all the congregation of the sons of Israel in the wilderness of Paran, at Kadesh; and they brought back word to them and to all the congregation and showed them the fruit of the land.

[27]Thus they told him, and said, "We went in to the land where you sent us; and it certainly does flow with milk and honey, and this is its fruit. [28] Nevertheless, the people who live in the land are strong, and the cities are fortified and very large; and moreover, we saw the descendants of Anak there. [29]Amalek is living in the land of the Negev and the Hittites and the Jebusites and the Amorites are living in the hill country, and the Canaanites are living by the sea and by the side of the Jordan."

[30]Then Caleb quieted the people before Moses and said, "We should by all means go up and take possession of it, for we will surely overcome it." [31]But the men who had gone up with him said, "We are not able to go up against the people, for they are too strong for us."

[32]So they gave out to the sons of Israel a bad report of the land which they had spied out, saying, "The land through which we have gone, in spying it out, is a land that devours its inhabitants; and all the people whom we saw in it are men of great size.

[33]There also we saw the Nephilim (the sons of Anak are part of the Nephilim); and we became like grasshoppers in our own sight, and so we were in their sight."

What happened when the Israelites failed to place their faith in God?
Numbers 14:1–19, NASB

[1]Then all the congregation lifted up their voices and cried, and the people wept that night. [2]All the sons of Israel grumbled against Moses and Aaron; and the whole congregation said to them, "Would that we had died in the land of Egypt! Or would that we had died in this wilderness! [3]Why is the LORD bringing us into this land, to fall by the sword? Our wives and our little ones will become plunder; would it not be better for us to return to Egypt?" [4]So they said to one another, "Let us appoint a leader and return to Egypt."

[5]Then Moses and Aaron fell on their faces in the presence of all the assembly of the congregation of the sons of Israel. [6]Joshua the son of Nun and Caleb the son of Jephunneh, of those who had spied out the land, tore their clothes; [7]and they spoke to all the congregation of the sons of Israel, saying, "The land which we passed through to spy out is an exceedingly good land. [8]If the LORD is pleased with us, then He will bring us into this land and give it to us—a land which flows with milk and honey.

[9]Only do not rebel against the LORD; and do not fear the people of the land, for they will be our prey. Their protection has been removed from them, and the LORD is with us; do not fear them." [10]But all the congregation said to stone them with stones. Then the glory of the LORD appeared in the tent of meeting to all the sons of Israel.

Moses Pleads for the People
[11]The LORD said to Moses, "How long will this people spurn Me? And how long will they not believe in Me, despite all the signs which I have performed in their midst? [12]I will smite them with pestilence and dispossess them, and I will make you into a nation greater and mightier than they."

[13]But Moses said to the LORD, "Then the Egyptians will hear of it, for by Your strength You brought up this people from their midst,

[14]and they will tell it to the inhabitants of this land. They have heard that You, O LORD, are in the midst of this people, for You, O LORD, are seen eye to eye, while Your cloud stands over them; and You go before them in a pillar of cloud by day and in a pillar of fire by night.

[15]Now if You slay this people as one man, then the nations who have heard of Your fame will say, [16]'Because the LORD could not bring this people into the land which He promised them by oath, therefore He slaughtered them in the wilderness.'

[17]But now, I pray, let the power of the LORD be great, just as You have declared, [18]'The LORD is slow to anger and abundant in loving-kindness, forgiving iniquity and transgression; but He will by no means clear the guilty, visiting the iniquity of the fathers on the children to the third and the fourth generations.'

[19]Pardon, I pray, the iniquity of this people according to the greatness of Your loving-kindness, just as You also have forgiven this people, from Egypt even until now."

Who is Joshua?
What happened when the Israelites failed to place their faith in God?
Numbers 14:20–45, NASB

20So the LORD said, "I have pardoned them according to your word; 21but indeed, as I live, all the earth will be filled with the glory of the LORD. 22Surely all the men who have seen My glory and My signs which I performed in Egypt and in the wilderness, yet have put Me to the test these ten times and have not listened to My voice, 23shall by no means see the land which I swore to their fathers, nor shall any of those who spurned Me see it. 24But My servant Caleb, because he has had a different spirit and has followed Me fully, I will bring into the land which he entered, and his descendants shall take possession of it. 25Now the Amalekites and the Canaanites live in the valleys; turn tomorrow and set out to the wilderness by the way of the Red Sea."

26The LORD spoke to Moses and Aaron, saying, 27"How long shall I bear with this evil congregation who are grumbling against Me? I have heard the complaints of the sons of Israel, which they are making against Me. 28Say to them, 'As I live,' says the LORD, 'just as you have spoken in My hearing, so I will surely do to you; 29your corpses will fall in this wilderness, even all your numbered men, according to your complete number from twenty years old and upward, who have grumbled against Me. 30Surely you shall not come into the land in which I swore to settle you, except Caleb the son of Jephunneh and Joshua the son of Nun

31Your children, however, whom you said would become a prey—I will bring them in, and they will know the land which you have rejected. 32But as for you, your corpses will fall in this wilderness. 33Your sons shall be shepherds for forty years in the wilderness, and they will suffer for your unfaithfulness, until your corpses lie in the wilderness.

34According to the number of days which you spied out the land, forty days, for every day you shall bear your guilt a year, even forty years, and you will know My opposition.

35I, the LORD, have spoken, surely this I will do to all this evil congregation who are gathered together against Me. In this wilderness they shall be destroyed, and there they will die.'"

36As for the men whom Moses sent to spy out the land and who returned and made all the congregation grumble against him by bringing out a bad report concerning the land, 37even those men who brought out the very bad report of the land died by a plague before the LORD. 38But Joshua the son of Nun and Caleb the son of Jephunneh remained alive out of those men who went to spy out the land.

Israel Repulsed

39When Moses spoke these words to all the sons of Israel, the people mourned greatly. 40In the morning, however, they rose up early and went up to the ridge of the hill country, saying, "Here we are; we have indeed sinned, but we will go up to the place which the LORD has promised." 41But Moses said, "Why then are you transgressing the commandment of the LORD, when it will not succeed? 42Do not go up, or you will be struck down before your enemies, for the LORD is not among you. 43For the Amalekites and the Canaanites will be there in front of you, and you will fall by the sword, inasmuch as you have turned back from following the LORD. And the LORD will not be with you." 44But they went up heedlessly to the ridge of the hill country; neither the ark of the covenant of the LORD nor Moses left the camp. 45Then the Amalekites and the Canaanites who lived in that hill country came down, and struck them and beat them down as far as Hormah.

Observations:

What does it say?

What does it mean?

How does it apply?

Notes and Discussion:

Project
Word Study

Notes and Discussion:

Numbers 21:4–8, NASB
The bronze serpent

[4]Then they set out from Mount Hor by the way of the Red Sea, to go around the land of Edom; and the people became impatient because of the journey.

[5]The people spoke against God and Moses, "Why have you brought us up out of Egypt to die in the wilderness? For there is no food and no water, and we loathe this miserable food."

[6]The LORD sent fiery serpents among the people and they bit the people, so that many people of Israel died. [7]So the people came to Moses and said, "We have sinned, because we have spoken against the LORD and you; intercede with the LORD, that He may remove the serpents from us." And Moses interceded for the people. [8]Then the LORD said to Moses, "Make a fiery serpent, and set it on a standard; and it shall come about, that everyone who is bitten, when he looks at it, he will live."

105

How does God use the Jordan River and Jericho to reveal glory?
How does God reveal Himself to a new generation through trials?
Joshua 3:1–13, NASB

[1]Then Joshua rose early in the morning; and he and all the sons of Israel set out from Shittim and came to the Jordan, and they lodged there before they crossed. [2]At the end of three days the officers went through the midst of the camp; [3]and they commanded the people, saying, "When you see the ark of the covenant of the LORD your God with the Levitical priests carrying it, then you shall set out from your place and go after it. [4]However, there shall be between you and it a distance of about 2,000 cubits by measure. Do not come near it, that you may know the way by which you shall go, for you have not passed this way before."

[5]Then Joshua said to the people, "Consecrate yourselves, for tomorrow the LORD will do wonders among you." [6]And Joshua spoke to the priests, saying, "Take up the ark of the covenant and cross over ahead of the people." So they took up the ark of the covenant and went ahead of the people.

[7]Now the LORD said to Joshua, "This day I will begin to exalt you in the sight of all Israel, that they may know that just as I have been with Moses, I will be with you. [8] You shall, moreover, command the priests who are carrying the ark of the covenant, saying, 'When you come to the edge of the waters of the Jordan, you shall stand still in the Jordan.'" [9]Then Joshua said to the sons of Israel, "Come here, and hear the words of the LORD your God."

[10]Joshua said, "By this you shall know that the living God is among you, and that He will assuredly dispossess from before you the Canaanite, the Hittite, the Hivite, the Perizzite, the Girgashite, the Amorite, and the Jebusite. [11]Behold, the ark of the covenant of the LORD of all the earth is crossing over ahead of you into the Jordan.

[12]Now then, take for yourselves twelve men from the tribes of Israel, one man for each tribe. [13]It shall come about when the soles of the feet of the priests who carry the ark of the LORD, the LORD of all the earth, rest in the waters of the Jordan, the waters of the Jordan will be cut off, and the waters which are flowing down from above will stand in one heap."

Observations:

What does it say?

What does it mean?

How does it apply?

Notes and Discussion:

Joshua 3:14–17, 4:1–14, NASB

[14]So when the people set out from their tents to cross the Jordan with the priests carrying the ark of the covenant before the people, [15]and when those who carried the ark came into the Jordan, and the feet of the priests carrying the ark were dipped in the edge of the water (for the Jordan overflows all its banks all the days of harvest), [16]the waters which were flowing down from above stood and rose up in one heap, a great distance away at Adam, the city that is beside Zarethan; and those which were flowing down toward the sea of the Arabah, the Salt Sea, were completely cut off. So the people crossed opposite Jericho. [17]And the priests who carried the ark of the covenant of the LORD stood firm on dry ground in the middle of the Jordan while all Israel crossed on dry ground, until all the nation had finished crossing the Jordan.

Memorial Stones from Jordan

[1]Now when all the nation had finished crossing the Jordan, the LORD spoke to Joshua, saying, [2]"Take for yourselves twelve men from the people, one man from each tribe, [3]and command them, saying, 'Take up for yourselves twelve stones from here out of the middle of the Jordan, from the place where the priests' feet are standing firm, and carry them over with you and lay them down in the lodging place where you will lodge tonight.'"

[4]So Joshua called the twelve men whom he had appointed from the sons of Israel, one man from each tribe; [5]and Joshua said to them, "Cross again to the ark of the LORD your God into the middle of the Jordan, and each of you take up a stone on his shoulder, according to the number of the tribes of the sons of Israel. [6]Let this be a sign among you, so that when your children ask later, saying, 'What do these stones mean to you?'

[7]then you shall say to them, 'Because the waters of the Jordan were cut off before the ark of the covenant of the LORD; when it crossed the Jordan, the waters of the Jordan were cut off.' So these stones shall become a memorial to the sons of Israel forever."

[8]Thus the sons of Israel did as Joshua commanded, and took up twelve stones from the middle of the Jordan, just as the LORD spoke to Joshua, according to the number of the tribes of the sons of Israel; and they carried them over with them to the lodging place and put them down there.

[9]Then Joshua set up twelve stones in the middle of the Jordan at the place where the feet of the priests who carried the ark of the covenant were standing, and they are there to this day. [10]For the priests who carried the ark were standing in the middle of the Jordan until everything was completed that the LORD had commanded Joshua to speak to the people, according to all that Moses had commanded Joshua. And the people hurried and crossed;

[11]and when all the people had finished crossing, the ark of the LORD and the priests crossed before the people.

[12]The sons of Reuben and the sons of Gad and the half-tribe of Manasseh crossed over in battle array before the sons of Israel, just as Moses had spoken to them; 13 about 40,000 equipped for war, crossed for battle before the LORD to the desert plains of Jericho.

[14]On that day the LORD exalted Joshua in the sight of all Israel; so that they revered him, just as they had revered Moses all the days of his life.

Who is Rahab?
How does God reveal Himself to a new generation through grace?
Joshua 5:13–15, Joshua 6:1–17, NASB

13Now it came about when Joshua was by Jericho, that he lifted up his eyes and looked, and behold, a man was standing opposite him with his sword drawn in his hand, and Joshua went to him and said to him, "Are you for us or for our adversaries?" 14He said, "No; rather I indeed come now as captain of the host of the LORD." And Joshua fell on his face to the earth, and bowed down, and said to him, "What has my lord to say to his servant?" 15The captain of the LORD's host said to Joshua, "Remove your sandals from your feet, for the place where you are standing is holy." And Joshua did so.

The Conquest of Jericho

1Now Jericho was tightly shut because of the sons of Israel; no one went out and no one came in. 2The LORD said to Joshua, "See, I have given Jericho into your hand, with its king and the valiant warriors.

3You shall march around the city, all the men of war circling the city once. You shall do so for six days. 4Also seven priests shall carry seven trumpets of rams' horns before the ark; then on the seventh day you shall march around the city seven times, and the priests shall blow the trumpets. 5It shall be that when they make a long blast with the ram's horn, and when you hear the sound of the trumpet, all the people shall shout with a great shout; and the wall of the city will fall down flat, and the people will go up every man straight ahead."

6So Joshua the son of Nun called the priests and said to them, "Take up the ark of the covenant, and let seven priests carry seven trumpets of rams' horns before the ark of the LORD."

7Then he said to the people, "Go forward, and march around the city, and let the armed men go on before the ark of the LORD."

8And it was so, that when Joshua had spoken to the people, the seven priests carrying the seven trumpets of rams' horns before the LORD went forward and blew the trumpets; and the ark of the covenant of the LORD followed them.

9The armed men went before the priests who blew the trumpets, and the rear guard came after the ark, while they continued to blow the trumpets. 10But Joshua commanded the people, saying, "You shall not shout nor let your voice be heard nor let a word proceed out of your mouth, until the day I tell you, 'Shout!' Then you shall shout!" 11So he had the ark of the LORD taken around the city, circling it once; then they came into the camp and spent the night in the camp.

12Now Joshua rose early in the morning, and the priests took up the ark of the LORD. 13The seven priests carrying the seven trumpets of rams' horns before the ark of the LORD went on continually, and blew the trumpets; and the armed men went before them and the rear guard came after the ark of the LORD, while they continued to blow the trumpets. 14Thus the second day they marched around the city once and returned to the camp; they did so for six days.

15Then on the seventh day they rose early at the dawning of the day and marched around the city in the same manner seven times; only on that day they marched around the city seven times. 16At the seventh time, when the priests blew the trumpets, Joshua said to the people, "Shout! For the LORD has given you the city.

17The city shall be under the ban, it and all that is in it belongs to the LORD; only Rahab the harlot and all who are with her in the house shall live, because she hid the messengers whom we sent.

Joshua 6:18–27, NASB

18But as for you, only keep yourselves from the things under the ban, so that you do not covet them and take some of the things under the ban, and make the camp of Israel accursed and bring trouble on it.

19But all the silver and gold and articles of bronze and iron are holy to the LORD; they shall go into the treasury of the LORD."

20So the people shouted, and priests blew the trumpets; and when the people heard the sound of the trumpet, the people shouted with a great shout and the wall fell down flat, so that the people went up into the city, every man straight ahead, and they took the city. 21They utterly destroyed everything in the city, both man and woman, young and old, and ox and sheep and donkey, with the edge of the sword.

22Joshua said to the two men who had spied out the land, "Go into the harlot's house and bring the woman and all she has out of there, as you have sworn to her."

23So the young men who were spies went in and brought out Rahab and her father and her mother and her brothers and all she had; they also brought out all her relatives and placed them outside the camp of Israel.

24They burned the city with fire, and all that was in it. Only the silver and gold, and articles of bronze and iron, they put into the treasury of the house of the LORD. 25However, Rahab the harlot and her father's household and all she had, Joshua spared; and she has lived in the midst of Israel to this day, for she hid the messengers whom Joshua sent to spy out Jericho.

26Then Joshua made them take an oath at that time, saying, "Cursed before the LORD is the man who rises up and builds this city Jericho; with the loss of his firstborn he shall lay its foundation, and with the loss of his youngest son he shall set up its gates." 27So the LORD was with Joshua, and his fame was in all the land.

Observations:

What does it say?

What does it mean?

How does it apply?

Who is Ruth?
How is God still at work during the time of the judges?
Judges, Ruth

"all the people did whatever seemed right in their own eyes."

Judges 21:25, NLT

Ruth 4:13–22, NASB

¹³So Boaz took Ruth, and she became his wife, and he went in to her. And the LORD enabled her to conceive, and she gave birth to a son.

¹⁴Then the women said to Naomi, "Blessed is the LORD who has not left you without a redeemer today, and may his name become famous in Israel.

¹⁵May he also be to you a restorer of life and a sustainer of your old age; for your daughter-in-law, who loves you and is better to you than seven sons, has given birth to him."

The Line of David Began Here

¹⁶Then Naomi took the child and laid him in her lap, and became his nurse. ¹⁷The neighbor women gave him a name, saying, "A son has been born to Naomi!" So they named him Obed. He is the father of Jesse, the father of David.

¹⁸Now these are the generations of Perez: to Perez was born Hezron, ¹⁹and to Hezron was born Ram, and to Ram, Amminadab, ²⁰and to Amminadab was born Nahshon, and to Nahshon, Salmon, ²¹and to Salmon was born Boaz, and to Boaz, Obed, ²²and to Obed was born Jesse, and to Jesse, David.

Notes and Discussion:

Judges, Ruth

The sons of Ruth

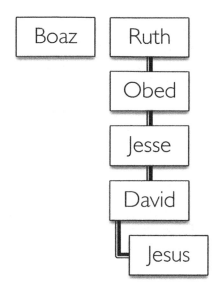

Observations:

Who is Saul?
What happens when Israel demands a king?
1 Samuel 9:1–2, NASB

1 Now there was a man of Benjamin whose name was Kish the son of Abiel, the son of Zeror, the son of Becorath, the son of Aphiah, the son of a Benjamite, a mighty man of valor. 2 He had a son whose name was Saul, a choice and handsome man, and there was not a more handsome person than he among the sons of Israel; from his shoulders and up he was taller than any of the people.

Notes and Discussion:

Observations on the life of Saul
1 Samuel 9:1–10:27, 1 Samuel 15:1–30

What does it say?

What does it mean?

How does it apply?

Notes and Discussion:

David to Christ

Foundations of Faith

Unit Essential Questions

1. How does God reveal and accomplish His mission from the time of David to Jesus?

2. How does understanding the progression of God's plan from David to Jesus impact my life?

Unit Learning Objectives

A. To understand how God continues to advance His mission to reflect His glory through His people, His temple and His covenant

B. To practice the skills of inductive bible study and exegetical conversations within community.

Unit Learning Assessments

1. Formative Quizzes

2. Summative Assessment

Daily Essential Questions

1. Who is David?

2. What is God's covenant with David?

3. Who is Solomon?

4. What happened to the northern tribes of Israel?

5. Who are Daniel and Esther?

6. Who are Ezra and Nehemiah?

7. Who is Isaiah?

8. Review: What have I learned?

9. Assessment Review: How will I demonstrate what I have learned?

From David to Christ

From Dedication to Desertion:

God expands His covenant with David, promising that the Messiah—who will reign for eternity—will come from his line. David's son then builds the temple that will be filled with the presence of God in the center of the land.

The temple of God is a working symbol of God's grace, glory and redemption to the nations of the earth.

But after dedicating the temple and the people to the LORD as instruments to spread His glory, the nation of Israel begins to distance themselves from God.

As the hearts of the people stray from God and their rebellion against Him grows, God keeps His promise and removes the people from their land.

With the temple destroyed and only a remnant of people remaining, God again begins to raise leaders who will not only return to the land, but will lead the people to return their hearts to God.

Then, when all seems lost, God raises prophets in the land who speak about the hope for a Messiah who will deliver God's people.

But before that day takes place, God continues to strategically go about His mission to fill the earth with His glory, preparing the world for the Messiah's coming.

Who is David?
How did God prepare another shepherd to lead His people?
I Samuel 17:1–11, NASB

¹Now the Philistines gathered their armies for battle; and they were gathered at Socoh which belongs to Judah, and they camped between Socoh and Azekah, in Ephes-dammim. ²Saul and the men of Israel were gathered and camped in the valley of Elah, and drew up in battle array to encounter the Philistines.

³The Philistines stood on the mountain on one side while Israel stood on the mountain on the other side, with the valley between them. ⁴Then a champion came out from the armies of the Philistines named Goliath, from Gath, whose height was six cubits and a span.

⁵He had a bronze helmet on his head, and he was clothed with scale-armor which weighed five thousand shekels of bronze. ⁶He also had bronze greaves on his legs and a bronze javelin slung between his shoulders.

⁷The shaft of his spear was like a weaver's beam, and the head of his spear weighed six hundred shekels of iron; his shield-carrier also walked before him

⁸He stood and shouted to the ranks of Israel and said to them, "Why do you come out to draw up in battle array? Am I not the Philistine and you servants of Saul? Choose a man for yourselves and let him come down to me. ⁹If he is able to fight with me and kill me, then we will become your servants; but if I prevail against him and kill him, then you shall become our servants and serve us." ¹⁰Again the Philistine said, "I defy the ranks of Israel this day; give me a man that we may fight together."

¹¹When Saul and all Israel heard these words of the Philistine, they were dismayed and greatly afraid.

Read I Samuel 17:12–58.

Observations:

What does it say?

What does it mean?

How does it apply?

Notes and Discussion:

What is God's covenant with David?
How does God's promise to David point us to Jesus?
2 Samuel 7:1–16, NASB

[1]Now it came about when the king lived in his house, and the LORD had given him rest on every side from all his enemies, [2]that the king said to Nathan the prophet, "See now, I dwell in a house of cedar, but the ark of God dwells within tent curtains." [3]Nathan said to the king, "Go, do all that is in your mind, for the LORD is with you."

[4]But in the same night the word of the LORD came to Nathan, saying, [5]"Go and say to My servant David, 'Thus says the LORD, "Are you the one who should build Me a house to dwell in?

[6]For I have not dwelt in a house since the day I brought up the sons of Israel from Egypt, even to this day; but I have been moving about in a tent, even in a tabernacle.

[7]Wherever I have gone with all the sons of Israel, did I speak a word with one of the tribes of Israel, which I commanded to shepherd My people Israel, saying, 'Why have you not built Me a house of cedar?'"

[8]"Now therefore, thus you shall say to My servant David, 'Thus says the LORD of hosts, "I took you from the pasture, from following the sheep, to be ruler over My people Israel.

[9]I have been with you wherever you have gone and have cut off all your enemies from before you; and I will make you a great name, like the names of the great men who are on the earth.

[10]I will also appoint a place for My people Israel and will plant them, that they may live in their own place and not be disturbed again, nor will the wicked afflict them any more as formerly,

[11]even from the day that I commanded judges to be over My people Israel; and I will give you rest from all your enemies. The LORD also declares to you that the LORD will make a house for you.

[12]When your days are complete and you lie down with your fathers, I will raise up your descendant after you, who will come forth from you, and I will establish his kingdom.

[13]He shall build a house for My name, and I will establish the throne of his kingdom forever.

[14]I will be a father to him and he will be a son to Me; when he commits iniquity, I will correct him with the rod of men and the strokes of the sons of men,

[15]but My loving-kindness shall not depart from him, as I took it away from Saul, whom I removed from before you.

[16]Your house and your kingdom shall endure before Me forever;

2 Samuel 7:18–29, NASB

David's Prayer

[18]Then David the king went in and sat before the LORD, and he said, "Who am I, O Lord GOD, and what is my house, that You have brought me this far? [19]And yet this was insignificant in Your eyes, O Lord GOD, for You have spoken also of the house of Your servant concerning the distant future. And this is the custom of man, O Lord GOD. [20]Again what more can David say to You? For You know Your servant, O Lord GOD!

[21]For the sake of Your word, and according to Your own heart, You have done all this greatness to let Your servant know. [22]For this reason You are great, O Lord GOD; for there is none like You, and there is no God besides You, according to all that we have heard with our ears. [23]And what one nation on the earth is like Your people Israel, whom God went to redeem for Himself as a people and to make a name for Himself, and to do a great thing for You and awesome things for Your land, before Your people whom You have redeemed for Yourself from Egypt, from nations and their gods?

[24]For You have established for Yourself Your people Israel as Your own people forever, and You, O LORD, have become their God. [25]Now therefore, O LORD God, the word that You have spoken concerning Your servant and his house, confirm it forever, and do as You have spoken, [26]that Your name may be magnified forever, by saying, 'The LORD of hosts is God over Israel'; and may the house of Your servant David be established before You.

[27]For You, O LORD of hosts, the God of Israel, have made a revelation to Your servant, saying, 'I will build you a house'; therefore Your servant has found courage to pray this prayer to You. [28]Now, O Lord GOD, You are God, and Your words are truth, and You have promised this good thing to Your servant. [29]Now therefore, may it please You to bless the house of Your servant, that it may continue forever before You. For You, O Lord GOD, have spoken; and with Your blessing may the house of Your servant be blessed forever."

Observations:

What does it say?

What does it mean?

How does it apply?

Who is Solomon?
How does God's temple reveal His glory and His plan for His people?
2 Chronicles 1:1-13, NASB

[1]Now Solomon the son of David established himself securely over his kingdom, and the LORD his God was with him and exalted him greatly.

[2]Solomon spoke to all Israel, to the commanders of thousands and of hundreds and to the judges and to every leader in all Israel, the heads of the fathers' households. [3]Then Solomon and all the assembly with him went to the high place which was at Gibeon, for God's tent of meeting was there, which Moses the servant of the LORD had made in the wilderness. [4]However, David had brought up the ark of God from Kiriath-jearim to the place he had prepared for it, for he had pitched a tent for it in Jerusalem. [5]Now the bronze altar, which Bezalel the son of Uri, the son of Hur, had made, was there before the tabernacle of the LORD, and Solomon and the assembly sought it out. [6]Solomon went up there before the LORD to the bronze altar which was at the tent of meeting, and offered a thousand burnt offerings on it.

[7]In that night God appeared to Solomon and said to him, "Ask what I shall give you."

Solomon's Prayer for Wisdom

[8]Solomon said to God, "You have dealt with my father David with great loving-kindness, and have made me king in his place. [9]Now, O LORD God, Your promise to my father David is fulfilled, for You have made me king over a people as numerous as the dust of the earth. [10]Give me now wisdom and knowledge, that I may go out and come in before this people, for who can rule this great people of Yours?" [11]God said to Solomon, "Because you had this in mind, and did not ask for riches, wealth or honor, or the life of those who hate you, nor have you even asked for long life, but you have asked for yourself wisdom and knowledge that you may rule My people over whom I have made you king, [12]wisdom and knowledge have been granted to you. And I will give you riches and wealth and honor, such as none of the kings who were before you has possessed nor those who will come after you." [13]So Solomon went from the high place which was at Gibeon, from the tent of meeting, to Jerusalem, and he reigned over Israel.

Observations:

2 Chronicles 5–6

The glory of God fills the temple of God

Observations:

What does it say?

What does it mean?

How does it apply?

Notes and Discussion:

What happened to the northern tribes of Israel?
How does proximity to the presence of God affect His people?
1 Kings 12:1–33, NASB

¹Then Rehoboam went to Shechem, for all Israel had come to Shechem to make him king. ²Now when Jeroboam the son of Nebat heard of it, he was living in Egypt (for he was yet in Egypt, where he had fled from the presence of King Solomon). ³Then they sent and called him, and Jeroboam and all the assembly of Israel came and spoke to Rehoboam, saying, ⁴"Your father made our yoke hard; now therefore lighten the hard service of your father and his heavy yoke which he put on us, and we will serve you." ⁵Then he said to them, "Depart for three days, then return to me." So the people departed.

⁶King Rehoboam consulted with the elders who had served his father Solomon while he was still alive, saying, "How do you counsel me to answer this people?" ⁷Then they spoke to him, saying, "If you will be a servant to this people today, and will serve them and grant them their petition, and speak good words to them, then they will be your servants forever." ⁸But he forsook the counsel of the elders which they had given him, and consulted with the young men who grew up with him and served him. ⁹So he said to them, "What counsel do you give that we may answer this people who have spoken to me, saying, 'Lighten the yoke which your father put on us'?" ¹⁰The young men who grew up with him spoke to him, saying, "Thus you shall say to this people who spoke to you, saying, 'Your father made our yoke heavy, now you make it lighter for us!' But you shall speak to them, 'My little finger is thicker than my father's loins! ¹¹Whereas my father loaded you with a heavy yoke, I will add to your yoke; my father disciplined you with whips, but I will discipline you with scorpions.'"

Observations:

What does it say?

What does it mean?

How does it apply?

How does proximity to the presence of God affect His people?
1 Kings 12:1–33, NASB

[12]Then Jeroboam and all the people came to Rehoboam on the third day as the king had directed, saying, "Return to me on the third day."[13]The king answered the people harshly, for he forsook the advice of the elders which they had given him, [14]and he spoke to them according to the advice of the young men, saying, "My father made your yoke heavy, but I will add to your yoke; my father disciplined you with whips, but I will discipline you with scorpions." [15]So the king did not listen to the people; for it was a turn of events from the LORD, that He might establish His word, which the LORD spoke through Ahijah the Shilonite to Jeroboam the son of Nebat.

The Kingdom Divided; Jeroboam Rules Israel
[16]When all Israel saw that the king did not listen to them, the people answered the king, saying,
"What portion do we have in David?
We have no inheritance in the son of Jesse;
To your tents, O Israel!
Now look after your own house, David!"

So Israel departed to their tents.[17]But as for the sons of Israel who lived in the cities of Judah, Rehoboam reigned over them.[18]Then King Rehoboam sent Adoram, who was over the forced labor, and all Israel stoned him to death. And King Rehoboam made haste to mount his chariot to flee to Jerusalem. [19]So Israel has been in rebellion against the house of David to this day.

[20]It came about when all Israel heard that Jeroboam had returned, that they sent and called him to the assembly and made him king over all Israel. None but the tribe of Judah followed the house of David.
[21]Now when Rehoboam had come to Jerusalem, he assembled all the house of Judah and the tribe of Benjamin, 180,000 chosen men who were warriors, to fight against the house of Israel to restore the kingdom to Rehoboam the son of Solomon.

[22]But the word of God came to Shemaiah the man of God, saying, [23]"Speak to Rehoboam the son of Solomon, king of Judah, and to all the house of Judah and Benjamin and to the rest of the people, saying, [24]'Thus says the LORD, "You must not go up and fight against your relatives the sons of Israel; return every man to his house, for this thing has come from Me." So they listened to the word of the LORD, and returned and went their way according to the word of the LORD.

Jeroboam's Idolatry
[25]Then Jeroboam built Shechem in the hill country of Ephraim, and lived there. And he went out from there and built Penuel. [26]Jeroboam said in his heart, "Now the kingdom will return to the house of David. [27]If this people go up to offer sacrifices in the house of the LORD at Jerusalem, then the heart of this people will return to their lord, even to Rehoboam king of Judah; and they will kill me and return to Rehoboam king of Judah." [28]So the king consulted, and made two golden calves, and he said to them, "It is too much for you to go up to Jerusalem; behold your gods, O Israel, that brought you up from the land of Egypt." [29]He set one in Bethel, and the other he put in Dan. [30]Now this thing became a sin, for the people went to worship before the one as far as Dan. [31]And he made houses on high places, and made priests from among all the people who were not of the sons of Levi. [32]Jeroboam instituted a feast in the eighth month on the fifteenth day of the month, like the feast which is in Judah, and he went up to the altar; thus he did in Bethel, sacrificing to the calves which he had made. And he stationed in Bethel the priests of the high places which he had made. [33]Then he went up to the altar which he had made in Bethel on the fifteenth day in the eighth month, even in the month which he had devised in his own heart; and he instituted a feast for the sons of Israel and went up to the altar to burn incense.

Jeremiah 52:1–11, NASB

The Fall of Jerusalem

Zedekiah was twenty-one years old when he became king, and he reigned eleven years in Jerusalem; and his mother's name was Hamutal the daughter of Jeremiah of Libnah. ²He did evil in the sight of the LORD like all that Jehoiakim had done. ³For through the anger of the LORD this came about in Jerusalem and Judah until He cast them out from His presence. And Zedekiah rebelled against the king of Babylon. ⁴Now it came about in the ninth year of his reign, on the tenth day of the tenth month, that Nebuchadnezzar king of Babylon came, he and all his army, against Jerusalem, camped against it and built a siege wall all around it.

⁵So the city was under siege until the eleventh year of King Zedekiah. ⁶On the ninth day of the fourth month the famine was so severe in the city that there was no food for the people of the land.

⁷ Then the city was broken into, and all the men of war fled and went forth from the city at night by way of the gate between the two walls which was by the king's garden, though the Chaldeans were all around the city. And they went by way of the Arabah. ⁸ But the army of the Chaldeans pursued the king and overtook Zedekiah in the plains of Jericho, and all his army was scattered from him. ⁹Then they captured the king and brought him up to the king of Babylon at Riblah in the land of Hamath, and he passed sentence on him. ¹⁰The king of Babylon slaughtered the sons of Zedekiah before his eyes, and he also slaughtered all the princes of Judah in Riblah. ¹¹Then he blinded the eyes of Zedekiah; and the king of Babylon bound him with bronze fetters and brought him to Babylon and put him in prison until the day of his death.

Observations:

What does it say?

What does it mean?

The destruction of the temple
Jeremiah 52:12–20, NASB

[12]Now on the tenth day of the fifth month, which was the nineteenth year of King Nebuchadnezzar, king of Babylon, Nebuzaradan the captain of the bodyguard, who was in the service of the king of Babylon, came to Jerusalem. [13]He burned the house of the LORD, the king's house and all the houses of Jerusalem; even every large house he burned with fire. [14]So all the army of the Chaldeans who were with the captain of the guard broke down all the walls around Jerusalem. [15]Then Nebuzaradan the captain of the guard carried away into exile some of the poorest of the people, the rest of the people who were left in the city, the deserters who had deserted to the king of Babylon and the rest of the artisans.

[16]But Nebuzaradan the captain of the guard left some of the poorest of the land to be vinedressers and plowmen.
[17]Now the bronze pillars which belonged to the house of the LORD and the stands and the bronze sea, which were in the house of the LORD, the Chaldeans broke in pieces and carried all their bronze to Babylon. [18]They also took away the pots, the shovels, the snuffers, the basins, the pans and all the bronze vessels which were used in temple service. [19]The captain of the guard also took away the bowls, the firepans, the basins, the pots, the lampstands, the pans and the drink offering bowls, what was fine gold and what was fine silver. [20]The two pillars, the one sea, and the twelve bronze bulls that were under the sea, and the stands, which King Solomon had made for the house of the LORD....

Observations:

What does it say?

What does it mean?

How does it apply?

Who are Daniel and Esther?
How does God preserve His people during their exile?
Daniel, Esther

Notes and Discussion:

Notes and Discussion:

Who are Ezra and Nehemiah?
How does God rebuild His temple and His city?
Nehemiah 2:11–3:22, 4:6, 4:14–16, NASB

[11]So I came to Jerusalem and was there three days. [12]And I arose in the night, I and a few men with me. I did not tell anyone what my God was putting into my mind to do for Jerusalem and there was no animal with me except the animal on which I was riding.

[13]So I went out at night by the Valley Gate in the direction of the Dragon's Well and on to the Refuse Gate, inspecting the walls of Jerusalem which were broken down and its gates which were consumed by fire.

[14]Then I passed on to the Fountain Gate and the King's Pool, but there was no place for my mount to pass.

[15]So I went up at night by the ravine and inspected the wall. Then I entered the Valley Gate again and returned.

[16]The officials did not know where I had gone or what I had done; nor had I as yet told the Jews, the priests, the nobles, the officials or the rest who did the work.

[17]Then I said to them, "You see the bad situation we are in, that Jerusalem is desolate and its gates burned by fire. Come, let us rebuild the wall of Jerusalem so that we will no longer be a reproach."

[18]I told them how the hand of my God had been favorable to me and also about the king's words which he had spoken to me. Then they said, "Let us arise and build." So they put their hands to the good work.

Nehemiah 2:11-18 (see 2:19-3:22)

[6]So we built the wall and the whole wall was joined together to half its height, for the people had a mind to work.

Nehemiah 4:6

[14]When I saw their fear, I rose and spoke to the nobles, the officials and the rest of the people: "Do not be afraid of them; remember the LORD who is great and awesome, and fight for your brothers, your sons, your daughters, your wives and your houses."

[15]When our enemies heard that it was known to us, and that God had frustrated their plan, then all of us returned to the wall, each one to his work.

[16]From that day on, half of my servants carried on the work while half of them held the spears, the shields, the bows and the breastplates; and the captains were behind the whole house of Judah.

Nehemiah 4:14-16

Observations:

How does God rebuild His temple and His city?
Ezra 3:1–13, NASB

[1]Now when the seventh month came, and the sons of Israel were in the cities, the people gathered together as one man to Jerusalem.

[2]Then Jeshua the son of Jozadak and his brothers the priests, and Zerubbabel the son of Shealtiel and his brothers arose and built the altar of the God of Israel to offer burnt offerings on it, as it is written in the law of Moses, the man of God. [3]So they set up the altar on its foundation, for they were terrified because of the peoples of the lands; and they offered burnt offerings on it to the LORD, burnt offerings morning and evening.

[4]They celebrated the Feast of Booths, as it is written, and offered the fixed number of burnt offerings daily, according to the ordinance, as each day required;

[5]and afterward there was a continual burnt offering, also for the new moons and for all the fixed festivals of the LORD that were consecrated, and from everyone who offered a freewill offering to the LORD.

[6]From the first day of the seventh month they began to offer burnt offerings to the LORD, but the foundation of the temple of the LORD had not been laid.

[7]Then they gave money to the masons and carpenters, and food, drink and oil to the Sidonians and to the Tyrians, to bring cedar wood from Lebanon to the sea at Joppa, according to the permission they had from Cyrus king of Persia.

Temple Restoration Begun
[10]Now when the builders had laid the foundation of the temple of the LORD, the priests stood in their apparel with trumpets, and the Levites, the sons of Asaph, with cymbals, to praise the LORD according to the directions of King David of Israel.

[11]They sang, praising and giving thanks to the LORD, saying, "For He is good, for His loving-kindness is upon Israel forever." And all the people shouted with a great shout when they praised the LORD because the foundation of the house of the LORD was laid. [12]Yet many of the priests and Levites and heads of fathers' households, the old men who had seen the first temple, wept with a loud voice when the foundation of this house was laid before their eyes, while many shouted aloud for joy, [13]so that the people could not distinguish the sound of the shout of joy from the sound of the weeping of the people, for the people shouted with a loud shout, and the sound was heard far away.

Observations:
Dialogue and Discussion

131

Who is Isaiah?
What is the messianic hope for the people of Israel?
Isaiah 11:1–12, NASB

[1]Then a shoot will spring from the stem of Jesse,
And a branch from his roots will bear fruit.

[2]The Spirit of the LORD will rest on Him,
The spirit of wisdom and understanding,
The spirit of counsel and strength,
The spirit of knowledge and the fear of the LORD.

[3]And He will delight in the fear of the LORD,
And He will not judge by what His eyes see,
Nor make a decision by what His ears hear;

[4]But with righteousness He will judge the poor,
And decide with fairness for the afflicted of the
earth; And He will strike the earth with the rod of
His mouth, And with the breath of His lips He will
slay the wicked.

[5]Also righteousness will be the belt about His loins,
And faithfulness the belt about His waist.

[6]And the wolf will dwell with the lamb,
And the leopard will lie down with the young goat,
And the calf and the young lion and the fatling
together; And a little boy will lead them.

[7]Also the cow and the bear will graze,
Their young will lie down together,
And the lion will eat straw like the ox.

[8]The nursing child will play by the hole of the
cobra,
And the weaned child will put his hand on the
viper's den.

[9]They will not hurt or destroy in all My holy
mountain,
For the earth will be full of the knowledge of the
LORD
As the waters cover the sea.

[10]Then in that day
The nations will resort to the root of Jesse,
Who will stand as a signal for the peoples;
And His resting place will be glorious.

The Restored Remnant

[11]Then it will happen on that day that the Lord
Will again recover the second time with His hand
The remnant of His people, who will remain, From
Assyria, Egypt, Pathros, Cush, Elam, Shinar,
Hamath,
And from the islands of the sea.

[12]And He will lift up a standard for the nations
And assemble the banished ones of Israel,
And will gather the dispersed of Judah
From the four corners of the earth.

Observations:

Notes

Dialogue and Discussion:

Review
What am I learning?
From David to Christ

Christ to Commission

Foundations of Faith

Unit Essential Questions

1. How does God reveal and accomplish His mission from the time of Christ to Commission?

2. How does understanding the progression of God's plan from Christ to Commission impact my life?

Unit Learning Objectives

A. To understand how God advances His mission to reflect His glory through the life, death and resurrection of Jesus Christ

B. To practice the skills of inductive bible study and exegetical conversations within community

Unit Learning Assessments

1. Formative Quizzes

2. Summative Assessment

Daily Essential Questions

1. Who is Zechariah?

2. Could Jesus have been the Messiah?

3. Did Christ claim to be the Messiah?

4. Did Christ's life meet the Messianic standard?

5. Why did Jesus die on a cross?

6. Did Jesus rise from the dead?

7. How do Christ's last words on earth reflect the eternal mission of God?

8. Review: What have I learned?

9. Assessment: How will I demonstrate what I have learned?

From Christ to Commission

Connecting the truth of God's revelation

When we view the Bible only in terms of separate Old and New Testaments, we risk missing the unity of God's revelation by creating an unnatural break in the story of God.

If the Bible were viewed as a drama, we would not see the Old Testament books as being Act 1, with an intermission before we pick up Act 2 in the New Testament books. Instead, we would view the time between Genesis 1–11 as a prologue or introduction, and Act 1 would be the time between the promise of God to Abraham in Genesis 12 and the fulfillment of that promise through the life, death, and resurrection of Jesus Christ found in John 21.

When we view Genesis 12 to the end of the Gospels as unit, then it's easier to understand the connection between Abraham and Christ. It's easier to understand the life and ministry of John the Baptist, whose life was dedicated to preparing the way for the Messiah. It's also easier to understand the anticipation that the nation of Israel has for the Messiah who will come and fulfill the promise. This messianic expectation for deliverance also helps us make sense of why the religious leaders of Christ's generation were so confused by His message. He was the Messiah spoken of in Isaiah, the Messiah that they needed. But the Messiah that they *wanted* was the one spoken of by the prophet Zechariah.

This connection between the fulfillment of God's promise to Abraham was even spoken of by Christ, when He used His last words from the cross to say, "It is finished." But while the redemptive act of Christ is complete, the mission of God to fill the earth with His glory will be the transition that will bring us into Act 2.

Silence and expectation

What is the silence?	What groups emerge during the silence?
	A.
Why does the silence matter?	
	B.
How does the silence prepare the way for Jesus?	C.
	D.

Who is Zechariah?
What was the messianic expectation at the time of Christ?

[9]Rejoice greatly, O daughter of Zion!
Shout in triumph, O daughter of Jerusalem!
Behold, your king is coming to you;
He is just and endowed with salvation,
Humble, and mounted on a donkey,
Even on a colt, the foal of a donkey.
Zechariah 9:9, NASB

[1]Behold, a day is coming for the LORD when the spoil taken from you will be divided among you. [2]For I will gather all the nations against Jerusalem to battle, and the city will be captured, the houses plundered, the women ravished and half of the city exiled, but the rest of the people will not be cut off from the city.

[3]Then the LORD will go forth and fight against those nations, as when He fights on a day of battle. [4]In that day His feet will stand on the Mount of Olives, which is in front of Jerusalem on the east; and the Mount of Olives will be split in its middle from east to west by a very large valley, so that half of the mountain will move toward the north and the other half toward the south. [5]You will flee by the valley of My mountains, for the valley of the mountains will reach to Azel; yes, you will flee just as you fled before the earthquake in the days of Uzziah king of Judah. Then the LORD, my God, will come, and all the holy ones with Him!

[6]In that day there will be no light; the luminaries will dwindle. [7]For it will be a unique day which is known to the LORD, neither day nor night, but it will come about that at evening time there will be light. [8]And in that day living waters will flow out of Jerusalem, half of them toward the eastern sea and the other half toward the western sea; it will be in summer as well as in winter.

[9]And the LORD will be king over all the earth; in that day the LORD will be the only one, and His name the only one. [10]All the land will be changed into a plain from Geba to Rimmon south of Jerusalem; but Jerusalem will rise and remain on its site from Benjamin's Gate as far as the place of the First Gate to the Corner Gate, and from the Tower of Hananel to the king's wine presses. [11]People will live in it, and there will no longer be a curse, for Jerusalem will dwell in security.
Zechariah 14:1–11, NASB

What does this mean?

Messianic Expectations

12Now this will be the plague with which the LORD will strike all the peoples who have gone to war against Jerusalem; their flesh will rot while they stand on their feet, and their eyes will rot in their sockets, and their tongue will rot in their mouth. 13It will come about in that day that a great panic from the LORD will fall on them; and they will seize one another's hand, and the hand of one will be lifted against the hand of another. 14Judah also will fight at Jerusalem; and the wealth of all the surrounding nations will be gathered, gold and silver and garments in great abundance. 15So also like this plague will be the plague on the horse, the mule, the camel, the donkey and all the cattle that will be in those camps.

16Then it will come about that any who are left of all the nations that went against Jerusalem will go up from year to year to worship the King, the LORD of hosts, and to celebrate the Feast of Booths.

17And it will be that whichever of the families of the earth does not go up to Jerusalem to worship the King, the LORD of hosts, there will be no rain on them. 18If the family of Egypt does not go up or enter, then no rain will fall on them; it will be the plague with which the LORD smites the nations who do not go up to celebrate the Feast of Booths. 19This will be the punishment of Egypt, and the punishment of all the nations who do not go up to celebrate the Feast of Booths.

20In that day there will be inscribed on the bells of the horses, "HOLY TO THE LORD." And the cooking pots in the LORD's house will be like the bowls before the altar. 21Every cooking pot in Jerusalem and in Judah will be holy to the LORD of hosts; and all who sacrifice will come and take of them and boil in them. And there will no longer be a Canaanite in the house of the LORD of hosts in that day.

Zechariah 14:12–21, NA

What were people looking for in their Messiah?

What did the people want?

Why did they think it was coming?

What did the people need?

Why were they not looking for it?

Could Jesus have been the Messiah?
The birth of Christ
Luke 2, NASB

²Now in those days a decree went out from Caesar Augustus, that a census be taken of all the inhabited earth. ²This was the first census taken while Quirinius was governor of Syria. ³And everyone was on his way to register for the census, each to his own city. ⁴Joseph also went up from Galilee, from the city of Nazareth, to Judea, to the city of David which is called Bethlehem, because he was of the house and family of David, ⁵in order to register along with Mary, who was engaged to him, and was with child. ⁶While they were there, the days were completed for her to give birth. ⁷And she gave birth to her firstborn son; and she wrapped Him in cloths, and laid Him in a manger, because there was no room for them in the inn.

⁸In the same region there were some shepherds staying out in the fields and keeping watch over their flock by night. ⁹And an angel of the Lord suddenly stood before them, and the glory of the Lord shone around them; and they were terribly frightened. ¹⁰But the angel said to them, "Do not be afraid; for behold, I bring you good news of great joy which will be for all the people; ¹¹for today in the city of David there has been born for you a Savior, who is Christ the Lord. ¹²This will be a sign for you: you will find a baby wrapped in cloths and lying in a manger." ¹³And suddenly there appeared with the angel a multitude of the heavenly host praising God and saying,.

¹⁴"Glory to God in the highest,
And on earth peace among men with whom He is pleased."

¹⁵When the angels had gone away from them into heaven, the shepherds began saying to one another, "Let us go straight to Bethlehem then, and see this thing that has happened which the Lord has made known to us." ¹⁶So they came in a hurry and found their way to Mary and Joseph, and the baby as He lay in the manger. ¹⁷When they had seen this, they made known the statement which had been told them about this Child. ¹⁸And all who heard it wondered at the things which were told them by the shepherds. ¹⁹But Mary treasured all these things, pondering them in her heart. ²⁰The shepherds went back, glorifying and praising God for all that they had heard and seen, just as had been told them.

Observations:

Was Jesus the Messiah?

The Word becomes flesh

A.   Jesus is the perfect reflection of _____ _____ (John 1:14).

B.   Jesus came to replace the law of _____ with the law of _____ (John 1:16–17).

C.   Moses and _____ _____ spoke about Jesus (John 1:45).

D.   Jesus came to _____ (Matthew 5:17–18).

E.   Those who strive to follow the law will be the ones _____.

  •   Matthew 16:21

  •   Matthew 20:18

  •   Luke 6:11

  •   Luke 19:47

F.   Jesus tells His disciples that John the Baptist was the fulfillment of _____.

  •   Malachi 4

  •   Matthew 17:10–13

Did Christ claim to be the Messiah?
The claim of Christ
John 2:13–25, 3:1–21, NASB

Cleansing the Temple on Passover

¹³The Passover of the Jews was near, and Jesus went up to Jerusalem. ¹⁴And He found in the temple those who were selling oxen and sheep and doves, and the money changers seated at their tables. ¹⁵And He made a scourge of cords, and drove them all out of the temple, with the sheep and the oxen; and He poured out the coins of the money changers and overturned their tables; ¹⁶and to those who were selling the doves He said, "Take these things away; stop making My Father's house a place of business." ¹⁷His disciples remembered that it was written, "Zeal for Your house will consume me." ¹⁸The Jews then said to Him, "What sign do You show us as your authority for doing these things?"

¹⁹Jesus answered them, "Destroy this temple, and in three days I will raise it up."

²⁰The Jews then said, "It took forty-six years to build this temple, and will You raise it up in three days?" ²¹But He was speaking of the temple of His body. ²²So when He was raised from the dead, His disciples remembered that He said this; and they believed the Scripture and the word which Jesus had spoken.

²³Now when He was in Jerusalem at the Passover, during the feast, many believed in His name, observing His signs which He was doing.

²⁴But Jesus, on His part, was not entrusting Himself to them, for He knew all men, ²⁵and because He did not need anyone to testify concerning man, for He Himself knew what was in man.

Reflection:

Knowing what we've learned from the Old Testament about the connection between the temple of God and the glory of God, what made the fact that this occurred on Passover even more significant?

Response:

Did Jesus claim to be God?

John 3:1–21, NASB

[1]Now there was a man of the Pharisees, named Nicodemus, a ruler of the Jews; [2]this man came to Jesus by night and said to Him, "Rabbi, we know that You have come from God as a teacher; for no one can do these signs that You do unless God is with him." [3]Jesus answered and said to him, "Truly, truly, I say to you, unless one is born again he cannot see the kingdom of God."

[4]Nicodemus said to Him, "How can a man be born when he is old? He cannot enter a second time into his mother's womb and be born, can he?" [5]Jesus answered, "Truly, truly, I say to you, unless one is born of water and the Spirit he cannot enter into the kingdom of God. [6]That which is born of the flesh is flesh, and that which is born of the Spirit is spirit.

[7]Do not be amazed that I said to you, 'You must be born again.'

[8]The wind blows where it wishes and you hear the sound of it, but do not know where it comes from and where it is going; so is everyone who is born of the Spirit."

[9]Nicodemus said to Him, "How can these things be?" [10]Jesus answered and said to him, "Are you the teacher of Israel and do not understand these things?

[11]Truly, truly, I say to you, we speak of what we know and testify of what we have seen, and you do not accept our testimony.

[12]If I told you earthly things and you do not believe, how will you believe if I tell you heavenly things? [13]No one has ascended into heaven, but He who descended from heaven: the Son of Man.

[14]As Moses lifted up the serpent in the wilderness, even so must the Son of Man be lifted up; [15]so that whoever believes will in Him have eternal life.

[16]"For God so loved the world, that He gave His only begotten Son, that whoever believes in Him shall not perish, but have eternal life.

[17]For God did not send the Son into the world to judge the world, but that the world might be saved through Him.

[18]He who believes in Him is not judged; he who does not believe has been judged already, because he has not believed in the name of the only begotten Son of God.

[19]This is the judgment, that the Light has come into the world, and men loved the darkness rather than the Light, for their deeds were evil.

[20]For everyone who does evil hates the Light, and does not come to the Light for fear that his deeds will be exposed.

[21]But he who practices the truth comes to the Light, so that his deeds may be manifested as having been wrought in God."

Observations:

How does it apply?

Did Christ's life meet the messianic standard?
The life of Christ
Luke 22: 1–23, NASB

Preparing the Passover

[1]Now the Feast of Unleavened Bread, which is called the Passover, was approaching. [2]The chief priests and the scribes were seeking how they might put Him to death; for they were afraid of the people.

[3]And Satan entered into Judas who was called Iscariot, belonging to the number of the twelve. [4]And he went away and discussed with the chief priests and officers how he might betray Him to them. [5]They were glad and agreed to give him money. [6]So he consented, and began seeking a good opportunity to betray Him to them apart from the crowd.

[7]Then came the first day of Unleavened Bread on which the Passover lamb had to be sacrificed. [8]And Jesus sent Peter and John, saying, "Go and prepare the Passover for us, so that we may eat it." [9]They said to Him, "Where do You want us to prepare it?" [10]And He said to them, "When you have entered the city, a man will meet you carrying a pitcher of water; follow him into the house that he enters. [11]And you shall say to the owner of the house, 'The Teacher says to you, "Where is the guest room in which I may eat the Passover with My disciples?"' [12]And he will show you a large, furnished upper room; prepare it there." [13]And they left and found everything just as He had told them; and they prepared the Passover.

The Lord's Supper

[14]When the hour had come, He reclined at the table, and the apostles with Him. [15]And He said to them, "I have earnestly desired to eat this Passover with you before I suffer; [16]for I say to you, I shall never again eat it until it is fulfilled in the kingdom of God." [17]And when He had taken a cup and given thanks, He said, "Take this and share it among yourselves; [18]for I say to you, I will not drink of the fruit of the vine from now on until the kingdom of God comes." [19]And when He had taken some bread and given thanks, He broke it and gave it to them, saying, "This is My body which is given for you; do this in remembrance of Me." [20]And in the same way He took the cup after they had eaten, saying, "This cup which is poured out for you is the new covenant in My blood. [21]But behold, the hand of the one betraying Me is with Mine on the table. [22]For indeed, the Son of Man is going as it has been determined; but woe to that man by whom He is betrayed!" [23]And they began to discuss among themselves which one of them it might be who was going to do this thing.

Did Christ's life meet the messianic standard?
The life of Christ
Luke 22: 39–44, NASB

The Garden of Gethsemane

39And He came out and proceeded as was His custom to the Mount of Olives; and the disciples also followed Him. 40When He arrived at the place, He said to them, "Pray that you may not enter into temptation." 41And He withdrew from them about a stone's throw, and He knelt down and began to pray, 42saying, "Father, if You are willing, remove this cup from Me; yet not My will, but Yours be done." 43Now an angel from heaven appeared to Him, strengthening Him. 44And being in agony He was praying very fervently; and His sweat became like drops of blood, falling down upon the ground.

Observations:

Read   What does it say?

Reflect   What does it mean?

Respond   How does it apply?

Why did Jesus die on a cross?
The death of Christ
John 19:14–30, NASB

¹⁴Now it was the day of preparation for the Passover; it was about the sixth hour. And he said to the Jews, "Behold, your King!" ¹⁵So they cried out, "Away with Him, away with Him, crucify Him!" Pilate said to them, "Shall I crucify your King?" The chief priests answered, "We have no king but Caesar."

¹⁶So he then handed Him over to them to be crucified. ¹⁷They took Jesus, therefore, and He went out, bearing His own cross, to the place called the Place of a Skull, which is called in Hebrew, Golgotha. ¹⁸There they crucified Him, and with Him two other men, one on either side, and Jesus in between.

¹⁹Pilate also wrote an inscription and put it on the cross. It was written, "JESUS THE NAZARENE, THE KING OF THE JEWS." ²⁰Therefore many of the Jews read this inscription, for the place where Jesus was crucified was near the city; and it was written in Hebrew, Latin and in Greek. ²¹So the chief priests of the Jews were saying to Pilate, "Do not write, 'The King of the Jews'; but that He said, 'I am King of the Jews.'" ²²Pilate answered, "What I have written I have written."

²³Then the soldiers, when they had crucified Jesus, took His outer garments and made four parts, a part to every soldier and also the tunic; now the tunic was seamless, woven in one piece. ²⁴So they said to one another, "Let us not tear it, but cast lots for it, to decide whose it shall be"; this was to fulfill the Scripture: "They divided My outer garments among them, and for My clothing they cast lots." ²⁵Therefore the soldiers did these things.

But standing by the cross of Jesus were His mother, and His mother's sister, Mary the wife of Clopas, and Mary Magdalene. ²⁶When Jesus then saw His mother, and the disciple whom He loved standing nearby, He said to His mother, "Woman, behold, your son!" ²⁷Then He said to the disciple, "Behold, your mother!" From that hour the disciple took her into his own household.

²⁸After this, Jesus, knowing that all things had already been accomplished, to fulfill the Scripture, said, "I am thirsty." ²⁹A jar full of sour wine was standing there; so they put a sponge full of the sour wine upon a branch of hyssop and brought it up to His mouth. ³⁰Therefore, when Jesus had received the sour wine, He said, "It is finished!" And He bowed His head and gave up His spirit.

Observations:

Why did Jesus die on Passover?
John 19:31–41, NASB

31Then the Jews, because it was the day of preparation, so that the bodies would not remain on the cross on the Sabbath (for that Sabbath was a high day), asked Pilate that their legs might be broken, and that they might be taken away. 32So the soldiers came, and broke the legs of the first man and of the other who was crucified with Him;

33but coming to Jesus, when they saw that He was already dead, they did not break His legs.
34But one of the soldiers pierced His side with a spear, and immediately blood and water came out. 35And he who has seen has testified, and his testimony is true; and he knows that he is telling the truth, so that you also may believe. 36For these things came to pass to fulfill the Scripture, "Not a bone of Him shall be broken." 37And again another Scripture says, "They shall look on Him whom they pierced."

38After these things Joseph of Arimathea, being a disciple of Jesus, but a secret one for fear of the Jews, asked Pilate that he might take away the body of Jesus; and Pilate granted permission. So he came and took away His body.

39Nicodemus, who had first come to Him by night, also came, bringing a mixture of myrrh and aloes, about a hundred pounds weight. 40So they took the body of Jesus and bound it in linen wrappings with the spices, as is the burial custom of the Jews.

41Now in the place where He was crucified there was a garden, and in the garden a new tomb in which no one had yet been laid. 42Therefore because of the Jewish day of preparation, since the tomb was nearby, they laid Jesus there.

Connecting the Truth

How does Jesus fulfill the requirements of the Old Testament Law?

Did Jesus rise from the dead?
The resurrection of Christ
John 20:1–18, NASB

[1]Now on the first day of the week Mary Magdalene came early to the tomb, while it was still dark, and saw the stone already taken away from the tomb. [2]So she ran and came to Simon Peter and to the other disciple whom Jesus loved, and said to them, "They have taken away the Lord out of the tomb, and we do not know where they have laid Him."

[3]So Peter and the other disciple went forth, and they were going to the tomb. [4]The two were running together; and the other disciple ran ahead faster than Peter and came to the tomb first; [5]and stooping and looking in, he saw the linen wrappings lying there; but he did not go in. [6]And so Simon Peter also came, following him, and entered the tomb; and he saw the linen wrappings lying there, [7]and the face-cloth which had been on His head, not lying with the linen wrappings, but rolled up in a place by itself. [8]So the other disciple who had first come to the tomb then also entered, and he saw and believed.

[9]For as yet they did not understand the Scripture, that He must rise again from the dead. [10]So the disciples went away again to their own homes.

[11]But Mary was standing outside the tomb weeping; and so, as she wept, she stooped and looked into the tomb; [12]and she saw two angels in white sitting, one at the head and one at the feet, where the body of Jesus had been lying.

[13]And they said to her, "Woman, why are you weeping?" She said to them, "Because they have taken away my Lord, and I do not know where they have laid Him."

[14]When she had said this, she turned around and saw Jesus standing there, and did not know that it was Jesus.

[15]Jesus said to her, "Woman, why are you weeping? Whom are you seeking?" Supposing Him to be the gardener, she said to Him, "Sir, if you have carried Him away, tell me where you have laid Him, and I will take Him away."

[16]Jesus said to her, "Mary!" She turned and said to Him in Hebrew, "Rabboni!" (which means, Teacher). [17]Jesus said to her, "Stop clinging to Me, for I have not yet ascended to the Father; but go to My brethren and say to them, 'I ascend to My Father and your Father, and My God and your God.'"

[18]Mary Magdalene came, announcing to the disciples, "I have seen the Lord," and that He had said these things to her.

Understanding the Resurrection

Why does it matter that Jesus rose from the dead?

How do we know that Jesus rose from the dead?

- Biblical evidence

- Circumstantial evidence

- Non-Christian evidence

How do Christ's last words on earth reflect the eternal mission of God?
The commission of Christ
Matthew 28:16–20, Acts 1:1–11, John 21:25, NASB

The Great Commission

[16]But the eleven disciples proceeded to Galilee, to the mountain which Jesus had designated. [17]When they saw Him, they worshiped Him; but some were doubtful. [18]And Jesus came up and spoke to them, saying, "All authority has been given to Me in heaven and on earth. [19]Go therefore and make disciples of all the nations, baptizing them in the name of the Father and the Son and the Holy Spirit, [20]teaching them to observe all that I commanded you; and lo, I am with you always, even to the end of the age."

John 21:25, NASB

[25]And there are also many other things which Jesus did, which if they were written in detail, I suppose that even the world itself would not contain the books that would be written.

Acts 1:1–11, NASB

[1]The first account I composed, Theophilus, about all that Jesus began to do and teach, [2]until the day when He was taken up to heaven, after He had by the Holy Spirit given orders to the apostles whom He had chosen. [3]To these He also presented Himself alive after His suffering, by many convincing proofs, appearing to them over a period of forty days and speaking of the things concerning the kingdom of God.

[4]Gathering them together, He commanded them not to leave Jerusalem, but to wait for what the Father had promised, "Which," He said, "you heard of from Me; [5]for John baptized with water, but you will be baptized with the Holy Spirit not many days from now."

[6]So when they had come together, they were asking Him, saying, "Lord, is it at this time You are restoring the kingdom to Israel?" [7]He said to them, "It is not for you to know times or epochs which the Father has fixed by His own authority;

[8]but you will receive power when the Holy Spirit has come upon you; and you shall be My witnesses both in Jerusalem, and in all Judea and Samaria, and even to the remotest part of the earth."

[9]And after He had said these things, He was lifted up while they were looking on, and a cloud received Him out of their sight. [10]And as they were gazing intently into the sky while He was going, behold, two men in white clothing stood beside them. [11]They also said, "Men of Galilee, why do you stand looking into the sky? This Jesus, who has been taken up from you into heaven, will come in just the same way as you have watched Him go into heaven."

Notes and Dialogue:

Observations:

What does it say?

What does it mean?

How does it apply?

Review
What am I learning?
From Christ to Commission

[3]Then Moses went up to God, and the LORD called to him from the mountain and said, "This is what you are to say to the descendants of Jacob and what you are to tell the people of Israel: [4]"You yourselves have seen what I did to Egypt, and how I carried you on eagles' wings and brought you to myself. [5]Now if you obey me fully and keep my covenant, then out of all nations you will be my treasured possession. Although the whole earth is mine, [6]you will be for me a kingdom of priests and a holy nation.' These are the words you are to speak to the Israelites."

Exodus 19:3–6, NASB

But you are a chosen people, a royal priesthood, a holy nation, God's special possession, that you may declare the praises of him who called you out of darkness into his wonderful light.

1 Peter 2:9, NASB

Commission to Culmination

Foundations of Faith

Unit Essential Questions

1. How does God reveal and accomplish His mission from the Commission to the present day?

2. How does understanding the progression of God's plan and His Commission impact my life?

Unit Learning Objectives

A. To understand how God continues to advance His mission to reflect His glory in the present day and how God will fulfill His promise, His Covenant and His mission

B. To practice the skills of inductive bible study and exegetical conversations within community

Unit Learning Assessments

1. Formative Quizzes

2. Summative Assessment

Daily Essential Questions

1. What is the church?

2. Who is the Holy Spirit?

3. How will it all end?

4. What have I learned?

From Commission to Culmination

Acts 2: 1–13, NASB

Pentecost

[1]When the day of Pentecost had come, they were all together in one place. [2]And suddenly there came from heaven a noise like a violent rushing wind, and it filled the whole house where they were sitting. [3]And there appeared to them tongues as of fire distributing themselves, and they rested on each one of them. [4]And they were all filled with the Holy Spirit and began to speak with other tongues, as the Spirit was giving them utterance.

[5]Now there were Jews living in Jerusalem, devout men from every nation under heaven. [6]And when this sound occurred, the crowd came together, and were bewildered because each one of them was hearing them speak in his own language.

[7]They were amazed and astonished, saying, "Why, are not all these who are speaking Galileans?

[8]And how is it that we each hear them in our own language to which we were born? [9]Parthians and Medes and Elamites, and residents of Mesopotamia, Judea and Cappadocia, Pontus and Asia, [10]Phrygia and Pamphylia, Egypt and the districts of Libya around Cyrene, and visitors from Rome, both Jews and proselytes,

[11]Cretans and Arabs—we hear them in our own tongues speaking of the mighty deeds of God." [12]And they all continued in amazement and great perplexity, saying to one another, "What does this mean?"

[13]But others were mocking and saying, "They are full of sweet wine."

What is the church?
How does God use His church to carry out His mission?
Acts 2:14–36, NASB
(see Acts 1:8, Acts 12, Acts 13, Ephesians 3:10)

14But Peter, taking his stand with the eleven, raised his voice and declared to them: "Men of Judea and all you who live in Jerusalem, let this be known to you and give heed to my words. 15For these men are not drunk, as you suppose, for it is only the third hour of the day; 16but this is what was spoken of through the prophet Joel:

17'And it shall be in the last days,' God says,
'That I will pour forth of My Spirit on all mankind; And your sons and your daughters shall prophesy, And your young men shall see visions, And your old men shall dream dreams;
18Even on My bondslaves, both men and women, I will in those days pour forth of My Spirit And they shall prophesy.
19'And I will grant wonders in the sky above
And signs on the earth below, Blood, and fire, and vapor of smoke.
20'The sun will be turned into darkness
And the moon into blood, Before the great and glorious day of the Lord shall come.
21'And it shall be that everyone who calls on the name of the Lord will be saved.'
22"Men of Israel, listen to these words: Jesus the Nazarene, a man attested to you by God with miracles and wonders and signs which God performed through Him in your midst, just as you yourselves know— 23this Man, delivered over by the predetermined plan and foreknowledge of God, you nailed to a cross by the hands of godless men and put Him to death. 24But God raised Him up again, putting an end to the agony of death, since it was impossible for Him to be held in its power. 25For David says of Him, 'I saw the Lord always in my presence; For He is at my right hand, so that I will not be shaken.

26'Therefore my heart was glad and my tongue exulted; Moreover my flesh also will live in hope;
27Because You will not abandon my soul to Hades, Nor allow Your Holy One to undergo decay. 28'You have made known to me the ways of life; You will make me full of gladness with Your presence.'

29"Brethren, I may confidently say to you regarding the patriarch David that he both died and was buried, and his tomb is with us to this day. 30And so, because he was a prophet and knew that God had sworn to him with an oath to seat one of his descendants on his throne, 31he looked ahead and spoke of the resurrection of the Christ, that He was neither abandoned to Hades, nor did His flesh suffer decay. 32This Jesus God raised up again, to which we are all witnesses. 33Therefore having been exalted to the right hand of God, and having received from the Father the promise of the Holy Spirit, He has poured forth this which you both see and hear. 34For it was not David who ascended into heaven, but he himself says:

'The Lord said to my Lord,
"Sit at My right hand,

35Until I make Your enemies a footstool for Your feet.'"

36Therefore let all the house of Israel know for certain that God has made Him both Lord and Christ—this Jesus whom you crucified."

Acts 2:14–36, NASB

Acts 2
The Church begins

The Ingathering

[37]Now when they heard this, they were pierced to the heart, and said to Peter and the rest of the apostles, "Brethren, what shall we do?" [38]Peter said to them, "Repent, and each of you be baptized in the name of Jesus Christ for the forgiveness of your sins; and you will receive the gift of the Holy Spirit. [39]For the promise is for you and your children and for all who are far off, as many as the Lord our God will call to Himself." [40]And with many other words he solemnly testified and kept on exhorting them, saying, "Be saved from this perverse generation!" [41]So then, those who had received his word were baptized; and that day there were added about three thousand souls.

[42]They were continually devoting themselves to the apostles' teaching and to fellowship, to the breaking of bread and to prayer.

[43]Everyone kept feeling a sense of awe; and many wonders and signs were taking place through the apostles. [44]And all those who had believed were together and had all things in common; [45]and they began selling their property and possessions and were sharing them with all, as anyone might have need. [46]Day by day continuing with one mind in the temple, and breaking bread from house to house, they were taking their meals together with gladness and sincerity of heart, [47]praising God and having favor with all the people. And the Lord was adding to their number day by day those who were being saved.

Acts 2:37–47, NASB

The Holy Spirit empowers

A. Jesus promises the Holy Spirit to live in and be with those who follow Him (John 14:16–18).

B. Jesus promises that the Holy Spirit will empower His followers to become His witnesses to the world (Acts 1:8).

C. What is the significance and the role of the Holy Spirit in the life of a Christ-centered theist?

Who is the Holy Spirit?
How does the Spirit of God empower His mission?
Acts 1:8

Notes:

The glory of God spreads

A.   The disciples carry out Christ's commission to the ends of the earth.

- Acts 4:31

- Acts 6:2

- Acts 6:7

- Acts 8:14

- Acts 11:1

- Acts 13:5

- Acts 17:13

- Acts 18:11

B.   For God so loved the world that He _____.

- What is _____ _____?

- What does it mean to _____?

- How do we _____God?

- How do we _____ Christians?

- How do we _____ non-Christians?

- The story of God's _____is called the _____.

How will it all end?
What is the culmination of God's mission on earth?
Revelation 7:9–10, NASB

9After these things I looked, and behold, a great multitude which no one could count, from every nation and all tribes and peoples and tongues, standing before the throne and before the Lamb, clothed in white robes, and palm branches were in their hands;

10and they cry out with a loud voice, saying, "Salvation to our God who sits on the throne, and to the Lamb."

Observation and Reflection:

How will it all end?
What is the culmination of God's mission on earth?
Revelation 21–22

Observations:

What does it say?

What does it mean?

How does it apply?

Notes and Discussion:

What have I learned?
How will I respond?
John 20:30–31, NASB

Why the Gospel was written

[30]Therefore many other signs Jesus also performed in the presence of the disciples, which are not written in this book; [31]but these have been written so that you may believe that Jesus is the Christ, the Son of God; and that believing you may have life in His name.

What Do I Believe?

Foundations of Faith

Unit Essential Questions

1. What have I learned?

2. What do I believe?

Unit Learning Objectives

A. To design and give a presentation that identifies and evaluates three critical concepts learned during this class

B. To demonstrate understanding and application of the essential questions of the class through a written exam

Unit Learning Assessments

1. Final Exam

2. Final Presentation

3. Combination

Final Assessment Options

	Option A. Final Exam	**Option B. Presentation**	**Option C. Combination**
1.	Review Unit 1	Assign presentations	Assign final assessments
2.	Review Unit 2	Student workday	Student workday
3.	Review Unit 3	Presentations	Presentations
4.	Review Unit 4	Presentations	Presentations
5.	Review Unit 5	Presentations	Presentations
6.	Self-assessments Cloud of Witnesses video	Self-assessments Cloud of Witnesses video	Review guide due Self-assessment
7.	Final exam	No final exam	Final exam

What are the foundations of Christ-centered faith?

The Foundational Questions	How does the Bible address the foundations of faith?
1. What is real?	
2. Who/what is God?	
3. Who is man?	
4. What is moral?	
5. What happens at death?	
6. What is the meaning of history?	
7. Why are we here?	

Assessment Review

Part I. Demonstrate knowledge

Part II. Demonstrate understanding

Part III. Demonstrate application

Examine ™

SPIRITUAL FORMATION TOOL

ChristCenteredDiscipleship.com

*"Everyone ought to examine themselves before they eat
of the bread and drink from the cup."*
1 Corinthians 11:28, NIV

Wheaton Press
Read. Respond. Reflect.™

Where are you?

Read. Respond. Reflect.

Directions: *Read through the verses below and highlight or underline any words or phrases that seem to reflect or resonate with where you are at.*

Skeptic. Presented with the person of Christ and the gospel multiple times, I demonstrate disinterest or unbelief.

"Even after Jesus had performed so many signs in their presence, they still would not believe in him." John 12:37, NIV

Characteristics: Calloused heart, dull ears, closed eyes.

"[F]or this people's heart has grown callous, their ears are dull of hearing, they have closed their eyes." Matthew 13:15a, WEB

Christ's Next-Step Invitation: Repent. Believe.

"Then he began to denounce the cities in which most of his mighty works had been done, because they didn't repent." Matthew 11:20, WEB

Growth Barrier: A lack of spiritual understanding.

"When anyone hears the message about the kingdom and does not understand it, the evil one comes and snatches away what was sown in their heart. This is the seed sown along the path." Matthew 13:19, NIV

Spiritual Need: A change of mind and heart initiated by the Holy Spirit, a loving and praying friend.

"He said to them, 'This kind can come out by nothing, except by prayer and fasting.'" Mark 9:29, WEB

"As for you, you were dead in your transgressions and sins, in which you used to live when you followed the ways of this world and of the ruler of the kingdom of the air, the spirit who is now at work in those who are disobedient." Ephesians 2:1-2, NIV

Seeker. Questioning, with a desire to learn more about Jesus.

"He answered, 'And who is he, sir? Tell me, so that I may believe in him.'" John 9:36, ISV

Characteristics: A ready heart, open ears, questions with an interest to learn more about Jesus.

"Again, the next day, John was standing with two of his disciples, and he looked at Jesus as he walked, and said, 'Behold, the Lamb of God!' The two disciples heard him speak, and they followed Jesus. Jesus turned, and saw them following, and said to them, 'What are you looking for?' They said to him, 'Rabbi' (which is to say, being interpreted, Teacher), 'where are you staying?' He said to them, 'Come, and see.' They came and saw where he was staying, and they stayed with him that day. It was about the tenth hour." John 1:35-39, WEB

Christ's Next-Step Invitation: Repent. Believe.

"Now after John was taken into custody, Jesus came into Galilee, preaching the Good News of God's Kingdom, and saying, 'The time is fulfilled, and God's Kingdom is at hand! Repent, and believe in the Good News.'" Mark 1:14-15, WEB

Growth Barrier: A lack of clear presentation and understanding of the gospel, a lack of invitation.

"How, then, can people call on someone they have not believed? And how can they believe in someone they have not heard about? And how can they hear without someone preaching?" Romans 10:14, ISV

Spiritual Need: A clear gospel presentation and an invitation to believe and receive salvation.

"But to all who did receive him, who believed in his name, he gave the right to become children of God." John 1:12, ESV

Believer. Presented with the gospel I believe.

"He said, 'Lord, I believe!' and he worshiped him." John 9:38, WEB

Characteristics: Seed begins to germinate, shallow soil, little or no roots.

Other seeds fell on rocky ground, where they did not have much soil, and immediately they sprang up, since they had no depth of soil, but when the sun rose they were scorched. And since they had no root, they withered away. Matthew 13:5-6

Christ's Next-Step Invitation: Follow.

"And he said to them, 'Follow me, and I will make you fishers of men.'" Matthew 4:19, ESV

Growth Barrier: Lack of roots, lack of knowledge, testing, trouble, persecution.

"These in the same way are those who are sown on the rocky places, who, when they have heard the word, immediately receive it with joy. They have no root in themselves, but are short-lived. When oppression or persecution arises because of the word, immediately they stumble. " Mark 4:16-17, WEB

Spiritual Need: Prayer, roots, knowledge, biblical teaching, time, worship and someone to walk with them.

"Like newborn infants, long for the pure spiritual milk, that by it you may grow up into salvation." 1 Peter 2:2, ESV

"So then, just as you received Christ Jesus as Lord, continue to live your lives in him, rooted and built up in him, strengthened in the faith as you were taught, and overflowing with thankfulness." Colossians 2:6-7, NIV

"We continually ask God to fill you with the knowledge of His will through all the wisdom and understanding that the Spirit gives, so that you may live a life worthy of the Lord and please Him in every way: bearing fruit in every good work, growing in the knowledge of God, being strengthened with all power according to His glorious might so that you may have great endurance and patience, and giving joyful thanks to the Father, who has qualified you to share in the inheritance of His holy people in the kingdom of light." Colossians 1:9-12, NIV

Follower. Growing in faith and love; deepening roots and knowledge; struggling with thorns, trials, forgiveness, doubt, and perseverance.

"By this all people will know that you are my disciples, if you have love for one another." John 13:35, ESV

Characteristics: Beginning to push through the soil, struggling with thorns and weeds.

"Others fell among thorns. The thorns grew up and choked them." Matthew 13:7, WEB

"And calling the crowd to him with his disciples, he said to them, 'If anyone would come after me, let him deny himself and take up his cross and follow me.'" Mark 8:34, ESV

Christ's Next-Step Invitation: Deny self; pick up cross; trust, obey, and love Christ and others.

"Then Jesus said to his disciples, "If anyone desires to come after me, let him deny himself, and take up his cross, and follow me." Matthew 16:24, WEB

Growth Barrier: Thorns, worries of this life, doubt, deceitfulness of wealth, comfort, self and self-will.

"Others are those who are sown among the thorns. These are those who have heard the word, and the cares of this age, and the deceitfulness of riches, and the lusts of other things entering in choke the word, and it becomes unfruitful." Mark 4:18-19

Spiritual Need: Deny self; trials; endurance, perseverance, time, small group relationships, and accountability.

"Consider it pure joy, my brothers and sisters, whenever you face trials of many kinds, because you know that the testing of your faith produces perseverance. Let perseverance finish its work so that you may be mature and complete, not lacking anything." James 1:2-4, NIV

"Through him we have also obtained access by faith into this grace in which we stand, and we rejoice in hope of the glory of God. Not only that, but we rejoice in our sufferings, knowing that suffering produces endurance, and endurance produces character, and character produces hope." Romans 5:2-4, ESV

"These have come so that the proven genuineness of your faith—of greater worth than gold, which perishes even though refined by fire—may result in praise, glory and honor when Jesus Christ is revealed." 1 Peter 1:7, NIV

Friend. Marked by obedient love for Christ and others; may wrestle with isolation, complacency and accountability.

"You are my friends if you do what I command you." John 15:14, ESV

Characteristics: Good soil, obedience to Christ, fruit, growing faith, increasing love and perseverance in trials.

"We ought always to thank God for you, brothers and sisters, and rightly so, because your faith is growing more and more, and the love all of you have for one another is increasing. Therefore, among God's churches we boast about your perseverance and faith in all the persecutions and trials you are enduring." 2 Thessalonians 1:3-4, NIV

Christ's Next-Step Invitation: Love, obey, go, teach.

"If you love me, you will keep my commandments." John 14:15, ESV

"Jesus came to them and spoke to them, saying, 'All authority has been given to me in heaven and on earth. Go, and make disciples of all nations, baptizing them in the name of the Father and of the Son and of the Holy Spirit, teaching them to observe all things that I commanded you. Behold, I am with you always, even to the end of the age.' Amen." Matthew 28:18-20

Growth Barrier: Complacency, fear, pride, lack of vision and lack of equipping.

"Then he said to his disciples, 'The harvest indeed is plentiful, but the laborers are few.'" Matthew 9:37, WEB

"How, then, can people call on someone they have not believed? And how can they believe in someone they have not heard about? And how can they hear without someone preaching?" Romans 10:14, ISV

Spiritual Need: Vision, continued obedience, equipping, empowerment, continued spurring and accountability within community.

"…to equip his people for works of service, so that the body of Christ may be built up until we all reach unity in the faith and in the knowledge of the Son of God and become mature, attaining to the whole measure of the fullness of Christ." Eph 4:12-13

"As for you, brothers, do not grow weary in doing good." 2 Thessalonians 3:13, ESV

"Let us continue to hold firmly to the hope that we confess without wavering, for the one who made the promise is faithful. And let us continue to consider how to motivate one another to love and good deeds, not neglecting to meet together, as is the habit of some, but encouraging one another even more as you see the day of the Lord coming nearer." Hebrews 10:23-25, ISV

Fisherman. Reflecting Christ and reproducing fruit of righteousness and good works.

"Because we have heard of your faith in Christ Jesus and of the love you have for all God's people—the faith and love that spring from the hope stored up for you in heaven and about which you have already heard in the true message of the gospel that has come to you. In the same way, the gospel is bearing fruit and growing throughout the whole world—just as it has been doing among you since the day you heard it and truly understood God's grace." Colossians 1:4-6, NIV

Characteristics: Good soil, fruitfulness, harvest, influence, reflecting Christ.

"Others fell on good soil, and yielded fruit: some one hundred times as much, some sixty, and some thirty." Matthew 13:8, WEB

Christ's Next-Step Invitation: Teach others.

"Therefore, as you go, disciple people in all nations, baptizing them in the name of the Father, and the Son, and the Holy Spirit, teaching them to obey everything that I've commanded you." Matthew 28:19-20a, ISV

Growth Barrier: Complacency, fear, pride, lack of vision, lack of equipping, weariness.

"Let's not get tired of doing what is good, for at the right time we will reap a harvest—if we do not give up." Galatians 6:9, ISV

"Think about the one who endured such hostility from sinners, so that you may not become tired and give up." Hebrews 12:3,

Spiritual Need: Perseverance, humility, faithfulness, accountability, reliable people.

"It gave me great joy when some believers came and testified about your faithfulness to the truth, telling how you continue to walk in it." 3 John 3, NIV

"And what you have heard from me in the presence of many witnesses entrust to faithful men who will be able to teach others also." 2 Timothy 2:2, ESV

Examine™ Spiritual Formation Planning Tool

More resources available at WheatonPress.com

Directions: Answer the following seven questions using the words or phrases that you highlighted or underlined.

1. Where am I?

Skeptic. When presented with the Gospel, I do not believe.

Seeker. Questioning, with a desire to learn more about Jesus.

Believer. Presented with the Gospel I chose to believe.

Follower. Growing in faith, love, and roots; struggling with thorns, trials and perseverance.

Friend. Marked by obedient love for Christ and others.

Fisherman. Reflecting Christ and bearing fruit of righteousness and good works.

2. Where would I like to be in six months?

Skeptic. When presented with the Gospel, I do not believe.

Seeker. Questioning, with a desire to learn more about Jesus.

Believer. Presented with the Gospel I chose to believe.

Follower. Growing in faith, love, and roots; struggling with thorns, trials and perseverance.

Friend. Marked by obedient love for Christ and others.

Fisherman. Reflecting Christ and bearing fruit of righteousness and good works.

3. What invitation do I need to respond to in order to take my next step?

Skeptic. Repent.

Seeker. Repent. Believe.

Believer. Follow.

Follower. Deny self. Pick up cross. Obey. Love Christ and others.

Friend. Love. Obey. Go.

Fisherman. Teach others.

4. What barriers will I face?

Skeptic. Calloused heart, deaf ears, closed eyes.

Seeker. Lack of clear testimony. Lack of invitation.

Believer. Lack of root. Testing. Trouble. Persecution.

Follower. Thorns. Worries of this life. Deceitfulness of wealth. Comfort. Self.

Friend. Complacency. Fear. Lack of vision. Lack of equipping.

Fisherman. Complacency. Fear. Lack of vision. Lack of equipping. Weariness.

5. What spiritual needs do I have?

Skeptic. Prayer. Repentance, A believing friend.

Seeker. Receive. Believe. Salvation.

Believer. Prayer. Roots. Knowledge. Teaching. Worship. Time.

Follower. Deny self. Trials. Endurance. Perseverance. Time. Small group relationships and accountability.

Friend. Vision. Continued obedience. Equipping. Opportunity. Empowerment. and accountability within community.

Fisherman. Perseverance. Faithfulness. Reliable people.

6. What steps will I take?

7. Who will I ask to hold me accountable?

Summary and Reflection

1. What did you find most interesting or surprising about your experience in this class?

2. What is one big idea that you want to take away from this class and apply to your life?

3. What did you find most challenging about this class?

4. What advice would you give to a student to help them get the most out of this class next year?

5   What steps do you want to take after this class is over to continue to develop a more complete understanding of the foundations for your own personal beliefs?

DUAL CREDIT FOR STUDENTS

Wheaton Press is excited to offer students the opportunity to receive dual credit for their Bible classes through a unique partnership with Colorado Christian University. Each Wheaton Press course has been recognized as the equivalent of a college-level class. As a result, Wheaton Press courses provide the opportunity for your students to receive dual credit.

Participating students will receive

• The opportunity to gain college credit during their normal course work at an affordable rate.

• College credits that are transferable to 90% of colleges and universities.*

About Colorado Christian University

• Colorado Christian University, a four-year Christian university located in Denver, Colorado, is fully accredited through the Higher Learning Commission of the North Central Association of Colleges and Schools.

• This means that credits are transferable to almost any school in the nation, including state universities and private colleges.

How students participate

When your students choose the dual-credit option they are able to earn three college credits for only $200 per class while they are taking their regular Bible Class.

Your students participate in the same assessments regardless of whether or not they participate. There is no extra work or assessments to receive the college credit in addition to the credit they will be receiving through your school.

This means that your students have the opportunity to enter college or university with up to 21 transferable college credits for only $1,400 over the course of four years.

Students pay the $200 course fee at the time of their registration at CCU. This course fee is paid directly to CCU and not to your school.

Students must earn a C or above to ensure that credit is valid at CCU or other colleges and universities.

*Note: Individual colleges and universities determine if they accept credit from Colorado Christian University.

In a recent survey conducted by CCU, over 90% of schools accepted their dual credit enrollment – including all public and private Christian universities surveyed.

Generally, the schools who did not accept their dual credit did not accept any form of college credit earned in high school – even AP credit.

Learn more at WheatonPress.com/DualCredit